GW01454848

MUTATIO

ART, CONSCIOUSNESS & THE ANTHROPOCENE

2024 ~ No. 0 | ISSN: 2766-2969

1   JEREMY JOHNSON
        Mutations, Imagination, and
        Futurability: An Introduction

14   BRANDT STICKLEY
        Approaching the Origin:
        The Diaphanous Body
        and Classical Chinese Medicine

35   SAM MICKEY
        Climate Crisis, Karma, Compassion

44   ANALOUISE KEATING
        Ontological Imagination:
        An Anzaldúan Manifesto
        for Social Change

53   MATTHEW SEGALL
        Manifesto of a Gaian Cosmology

63   BARBARA KARLSON
        Becoming Metamorphic
        Moving Towards a New Conception of Life

71   SEAN KELLY
        Revisiting *Coming Home*

INTEGRAL IMPRINT

Contributors to this issue:

ANALOUISE KEATING, professor of Multicultural Women's & Gender Studies at Texas Woman's University, is a published authority on Latina authors, African-American literature, queer studies, multiculturalism, 18th- and 19th-century American writers, feminist theory, and pedagogy.

Dr. BARBARA KARLSEN is a Continuum Movement Teacher, Somatic Psychotherapist, and Somatic Re-birther, who holds a certificate in Psychedelic assisted therapy from Naropa University. Barbara has a private practice in Marin County, CA.

BRANDT STICKLEY, Associate Professor in the College of Classical Chinese Medicine, National University of Natural Medicine, pursues a synthesis of Classical Han and Tang Dynasty herbal medicine and acupuncture, Chinese magical medicine, philosophy and religion, with concepts of psychosomatic medicine, body-oriented psychology, neuro-phenomenology, process-oriented philosophy, imaginal, integral, and consciousness studies.

JEREMY JOHNSON, a writer and philosopher living in southern Vermont, is the author of *Seeing Through the World: Jean Gebser and Integral Consciousness* (2019), and *Fragments of an Integral Future* (2025). Jeremy advocates new forays into ecological thought and planetary futuring.

MATTHEW SEGALL PhD—Associate Professor in the Philosophy, Cosmology, and Consciousness Program at CIIS in San Francisco and Chair of the Science Advisory Committee for the Cobb Institute—is a transdisciplinary researcher, writer, teacher, and philosopher applying process-relational thought across the natural and social sciences, as well as to the study of consciousness.

SAM MICKEY PhD, is an author and educator working at the intersection of philosophical, religious, and scientific perspectives on human-Earth relations. He is a research associate at the Yale Forum on Religion and Ecology and an adjunct professor in the Theology and Religious Studies department at the University of San Francisco.

SEAN KELLY is Professor of Philosophy, Cosmology, and Consciousness at the California Institute of Integral Studies (CIIS). Along with his more academic pursuits, Sean has trained intensively in the Chinese internal arts and has been teaching taiji since 1990. He has worked closely with Joanna Macy and is a trained facilitator in The Work that Reconnects.

JEREMY JOHNSON

Mutations, Imagination, and Futurability: An Introduction

Mutations Issue Zero

MUTATIONS: ZERO ENTERS TIME ORTHOGONALLY. Lately, time has felt more like a broken rhythm. Clock-time was already wavering, a thin trance waiting to be liberated from the speed of capital. In its place, time has become a strange pluralism. It rushes forward and stands still. Time is the heaviness we feel about uncertain climate futures, and the weightless flurry of all our transient nows. Time shows up as the rote pulse of calendar app notifications, now robbed of any sense of urgency during the blurry weeks of COVID lockdown, but we all feel that a different order of time has come *alive* in its place—a torrent dramatic and full, roaring with the import of historical, political and planetary events. Mutations of language concerning this emergent consciousness of time have proliferated. With new temporal sensibilities come new senses of world, self, and being, and so there are the great lists of proclaimed epochs attempting to name the when and the where of our arrival: Anthropocene, Chthulucene, Capitolocene, really "a (hi)story with a thousand names," and "The Infinity of the Anthropocene."[1]

The present array of epoch-naming speaks to a certain recognition, a new structure of feeling showing up in public conversations like the gloomy ambience of an Anthropocene track. We no longer ask, "how is the weather?" without that track pervading the space between words. Time makes an appearance in those interstices, too: a subtle recognition, a certain anxiousness, perhaps even a sense of guilt that *although we are already living in new a time, demanding a new worldview, we do not know how to address this remarkable new realism.*

Stated poetically, because it often through poetry and imagination where we first find language adequate enough to begin voicing this planetary intensification: we have begun to trace, in the very bones of our being, the contours of a new worldview.

The theme of time stitches together every fiber of Anthropocene living. Whenever we circumambulate the loaded subject of climate in conversation, we intuitively grok French philosopher Paul Valéry's now well-worn aphorism, "the future… is no longer quite what what it used to be."[2] That line has become something like a melancholic track, stuck on repeat. When we name this slippery feeling, call it a "climate melancholia," the naming reveals something about the entangled relations between time, capital and climate (i.e., Capitolocene), but it also discloses characteristics of the *new* time that has already begun to shape our social imaginaries.

Franco Bifo Berardi, in his 2011 book *After The Future,* called it the "slow cancellation of the future," bringing attention to the underlying metaphysical and mythological assumptions our culture makes about the nature and direction of time itself.[3] The moderns, or those who were "pervaded by a religious belief in the future" (a future often involving the unending development of capital), have ultimately lost faith in their utopias of tomorrow.[4] Whereas the early twentieth century could be characterized by Italian Futurists like Filippo Tommaso Marinetti and his poetic glorification of the newly invented race car—"god of a race of steel … drrrunken on space"(!)—we, the inhabitants of the present, no longer imbue the future with an electro-utopian aura.[5] The digital age arrived, but it did not bring about the emancipation of labor. The cultural sensibility of the moderns, those who imagined that time was like a race car, powering the brilliantine engine of capital, has receded in favor of a wilder realism.

It is this wilder realism which enters time orthogonally. The structure of feeling pervading our culture already acknowledges the arrival of this new time.

"The music we grew up with," a distorted radio voice states on a recent Oneohtrix Point Never track, "doesn't speak for us in the new era we're now going through… now, simply, we all grew up to be something new."[6] If the very particular, and very modern consciousness of time and the future has receded from the horizon of our being, it is because we already find ourselves in a *mutational* process of realizing new forms of being, both within and without.

Planetary conditions have readily testified to this radical transparency. "At any given moment," Andreas Malm wrote in *The Progress of This Storm: Nature and Society in a Warming World*, "the excess of heat in the earth system is the sum of all those historical fires… the storm of climate change draws its force from countless acts of combustion… We can never be in the heat of the moment, only the heat of this ongoing past… indeed, the air is heavy with time."[7]

Each planetary event—whether climatological or viral—arrives like an emissary from the future, offering lessons like crystalline fragments belonging to the whole of time.

Climate uniquely intensifies and catalyzes this new consciousness in ways that neither Marinetti's race car nor stuck-in-forward-gear capitalist time ever could. When we approach the subject of climate through the singularity of events like heat domes or hurricanes, we encounter a radically transparent temporality where present is always-already "dissolving into past and future alike."[8]

Another fragment from the future arrives with this insight. The past erupts in the fiery heat of the present (quite literally in cases like the recent wildfires of the Pacific Northwest and Australia). The future holds a spooky intimacy with us too, enmeshed as unborn generations latently are in the activities of our present. Anthropocene time marks the annunciation of *weird* (as in *twisted*) time, uncanny time: it stretches, folds and enfolds in marvelous entanglements as if it were all happening at once—and it is.

Like entering the "Zone" in Andrei Tarkovsky's 1979 film *Stalker*, weird time can never be approached directly. The shape of time takes on manifold forms—spirals, weaves and rhizomes, naming just a few—in order to accommodate these complex, processual, ever-intensifying ecological and climatological relationships.

Weird time cannot be evaded. Transparency is found already in and through every step, every turn we make.

Reversals

Eco-philosopher Timothy Morton made this point when he collaborated with artist Justin Brice Guariglia to display "eco-haikus" in public spaces: "WE ARE THE ASTEROID."[9] It is a provocative way of communicating Anthropocene weirdness, the uncomfortable realization that humans are responsible for the sixth great extinction. Another eco-haiku goes, "WARNING: HUMAN HURRICANE," and then the next goes for the explicitly temporal: "FOR SYMBIOSIS: REDUCE SPEED NOW."[10]

When we linger we create time and relationships bloom. Unrelenting haste severs relationship, and like German philosopher Byung-Chul Han talks about, a culture driven so one-sidedly by haste creates the conditions for its own atomization—in the univocal embrace of haste, we lose space *and* time. We are no longer familiar enough with the pace of living relationship. The "scent of time," like Proust's madeleine, can only be known by slowing down, growing into the fullness of time through our senses.

"Utopia has been yang," Ursula K. Le Guin wrote, comparing the culture of the moderns to the masculinity of the yang concept in Chinese philosophy, "the big yang motorcycle trip… firm, active, aggressive, lineal, progressive, creative, expanding… our civilization is now so intensely yang that any imagination of bettering its injustices or eluding its self-destructiveness must involve a reversal." Slow down and reversal does not necessarily mean *linear* retrogrades, a mere gear shift, retreating back down the road we came. They form a movement into new orders of being where our previous conceptions no longer make sense. Marshall McLuhan understood this too. "The greatest of all reversals," he wrote in *Understanding Media*, took place with the new electronic culture, which "ended sequence by making things instant."[11] Orthogonal time breaks in. "That great pattern of being," McLuhan contemplated, "that reveals new and opposite forms just as the earlier forms reach their peak performance… from lineal connections to configurations."[12] As the total colonization of time and the human being into algorithm is occurring, and even as "remarkable" innovations of financial capital continue unabated, a new order of being has already set in.[13]

This reversal, which is to say this emergent worldview, appears to involve:

a) The breaking free of time from "clock-time," and the constraints capital in the old worldview

b) The resurgence and intensification of time through climatological and ecological realities, which in turn catalyze in us a new consciousness of time

c) The catastrophic collapse of our modernist worldview, creating a sense of *mutational urgency*, and necessitating an orthogonal move into cultural practices aligned with biospheric constraints: i.e., bioregionalism, peer-to-peer economics, and regenerative principles which decenter the human within a more cooperative "Gaianthropic" view[14]

d) This orthogonal move involves the mutational leap from abstract, extractive *globalization* to concretizing and regenerative *"planetization"*

While the latter two points exhibit our new reality, and their existential gravity cannot be overstated, their realization in and through cultural evolution is remains prefigurative. Emissaries from the future continue to arrive in the form of catastrophe. They intensify and catalyze new mutations of thought and imagination.

Our culture operates anachronistically in that even as we are shaped by the new structure of feeling, tomorrow's *being*, we continue to act from a *knowing* that belongs to yesterday. McLuhan, again, put it ever so succinctly: "We look at the present through a rear-view mirror. We march backwards into the future."[15]

Historian of consciousness William Irwin Thompson recognized the initiatory potential that such disruptions can have on cultural transformation. "Catastrophes," he wrote, "are discontinuous transitions in Culture-Nature through which knowing has an opening to Being," and so with any of these future fragments and orthogonal arrivals we might obtain momentary glimpses of tomorrow. These glimpses crystallize new pathways between our being and knowing, "a rapid flip-over or reversal in which the unthinkable becomes possible."[16]

When our knowing and being are rendered transparent to one another, the future is present, even fulfilled to some immeasurable degree through our participation.

When we move from the broad shape of cultural evolution and consider the life of an individual, orthogonal time shows up in the intensification of the spiritual present. The present aids us in forgoing the compulsive atomization of speed and the segmenting linearity of machine time, both of which only serve to divide ourselves and the world.

It is through the spiritual present that we can act from a more intelligible and "senseful" awareness that cultivates a friendlier consciousness of time and blossoms forth in us: not a fragment, no, but the sudden "flashing-forth" through the whole of time.[17] This form of intensified presence alone appears sufficiently luminous enough to render the integrality of our world—with its living relationships in the radiant body of time—at last cohered, visible and transparent.

Mutant Imaginations and Futurability

Another fragment from the ever-present future arrives through considering the symbiotic relationships that constitute our being. Complex intelligence, we are learning, shows up everywhere, from cephalopods to slime molds, or the mycelial networks of fungi. *We* are a strange pluralism, too, with bacteria making up more than half of our body's cells.[18] Science fiction imaginaries are helping us to wrestle with this transparency, and as Arkady Martine so effectively queried in her recent fiction — *"how wide is the concept of you?"*[19] Each of us, then, is "already a symbiotic being entangled with other symbiotic beings."[20]

For the old worldview this entanglement feels like an almost unbearable transparency, but like the warming of climate and the intensification of time, it foments in us a potent mutational urgency.[21] Kim Stanley Robinson has recently emphasized the catalytic and mutational import these realizations have on our culture: "to survive you depend on any number of interspecies operations going on within you all at once. We are societies made of societies; there are nothing but societies. This is shocking news—it demands a whole new world view."[22]

Fortunately, we find ourselves already standing (or crawling, slithering, fluttering) in a new time, the "thick present" anthropologist Donna Haraway named, "a temporality of the thick, fibrous, and lumpy 'now' which is ancient and not... a tentacular web of troubling relations that matter now."[23] Descriptions like these are not definitive or totalizing. They are inquisitive and open. Mutagenic and creative matrixes that help us relate with a living world that is always relating with us.

Berardi suggests the concept of "futurability," which provides a helpful framing for *Mutations* as a creative and time-emancipating project. "Futurability refers to the multidimensionality of the future: in the present a plurality of futures is inscribed," he writes, emphasizing that futurability is really the embrace of that wider and *wilder* time, the time of "becoming other" through creative actualization of futures "already inscribed in the present."[24] Berardi echoes the words of Swiss poet and phenomenologist of consciousness Jean Gebser (1905-1973). "Our concern," Gebser remarked in 1949, "is to render transparent everything latent "behind" and "before" the world—to render transparent our own origin, our entire human past, as well as the present, which already contains the future. We are shaped and determined not only by today and yesterday, but by tomorrow as well."[25]

The word "mutation" is borrowed from Gebser, who wrote about the transformational leaps of time, art, and language across the history of consciousness. Of special import for Gebser was the "integral" mutation, the emergence of a transparent and "aperspectival world," which he considered already well underway in the twentieth century.

This new mutation, succinctly, involved a fundamental leap:

1. From space and abstract thinking to time, processual thinking (thinking *with* time), and "senseful" awaring

2. overcoming the many reified dualisms (human/non-human, self/other, past/future, life/death) through

3. a realization of the new ontological ground, *transparency*: a consciousness of the whole which in turn makes the previous two characteristics possible. Transparency has created the necessary preconditions for an integrative process to take place. Or stated explicitly: the *regeneration* of the whole history of consciousness (all previous mutations), which must be rendered whole and co-effectual through the ineradicable present if we are to realize the future (the integral mutation).

What utterance in language could sufficiently speak to this new consciousness of time, this weirding of time in to entangled threads of living relations—past, present, and future? How do mutations of consciousness and culture help us to make that orthogonal move into habitable futures?

It is this inquiry into new ontological possibilities, ecological, processual, or imaginal in nature, that many of the contributors to *Mutations* journal are writing about. Our journal is humbly seeking to continue the fundamental inquiry of Gebser's *kulturphilosophie*: answering the call of a *mutational urgency*, attempting to creatively participate with futures that have already arrived and continue to shape the present.

Mutations seeks to give voice, shape, and form to these fragments of latent-but-present futures, body them forth through new language, art, scholarship and even "planetary" imaginaries.[26] If we are to have any futurability, if we wish to reclaim the future and therefore emancipate time from its capture by colonization, capital and labor, it must be through an orthogonal move into new and intensified forms of consciousness and imagination—it really is mutants or bust.

The *integral* mutation, then, concerns an orthogonal move into new ontologies of space and time, commingling with a revivified spiritual imagination, cohering new and habitable planetary futures. The title for Issue Zero, "Art, Consciousness and the Anthropocene," is a variation of this transformational triptych:

I.   **imagination (art):** the creative process of shaping new futures, remediating ancestral histories, realizing them through aesthetics, storytelling, and other cultural expressions.
II. **mutations (consciousness):** the history of consciousness and cultural evolution actively shapes us in the present. When we clarify their histories—even trace the origins of our "modern" worldview to its respective consciousness structure—we can ameliorate the sense of vertigo during this interregnum period, teasing the threads of the old worldview from the new.
III. **and futurability (Anthropocene):** when we participate in new possibilities of time and space, self and world, we necessarily engage with creative imagination and give these new possibilities their language, art, and concepts, i.e., their historical forms. Fragments of the future bloom in the present. The two previous themes fold into a third. "Futurability," the creative participation with and realization of habitable futures through the radiant transparency of the intensified present.

Mutations, imagination, futurability. Cultural evolution initiates us into this moment of dramatic bifurcation between one world closing down and planetary futures calling us home. We can feel it in ourselves, brimming over as we are with mutational urgency: a leap is needed, a consciousness of the whole, integral human being that can meet civilizational crisis with emergent forms of planetary "transindividuation."[27] Not the exhausted and partial expression of the human-as-modern, which has already concluded itself, but the transparent human who can engage with the "unthinkable" present of the Anthropocene because they recognize it as a mirror and creative invitation into their own knowing and being.[28]

It is through that unthinkable present, like an emptiness that is in reality very alive, and very full, that we are learning to "become a silence that calls the future."[29]

Mutants of Issue Zero

Brandt Stickley initiates our volume with a meditation on embodiment through a remedial consideration of integral consciousness and the body-as-time. "Contained within this three-dimensional embodiment," Stickley writes, "we may also uncover the seeds of time-freedom as fourth-dimensionality."

In "Climate Crisis, Karma, Compassion," Sam Mickey challenges our propensity to reinvent anthropocentric thinking. Rather than accruing more "karma" through our dualistic fixations, which continue to frame humanity-against-biosphere narratives, Mickey suggests a more compassionate and even mutational response to the climate crisis involves resting in "coexistentialism" with our planetary kin. This coexistential turn recognizes that "it is only through the inhuman that humankind can grow forth."

AnaLouise Keating articulates the central role and ontological status, that imagination itself holds for social transformation in the new mutation: "The Ontological Imagination: An Anzaldúan Manifesto for Social Change." Drawing from the posthumously published work of queer feminist and visionary scholar Gloria Anzaldúa (*Light in the Dark/Luz en lo oscuro: Rewriting Identity, Spirituality, Reality*), Keating proposes that the "ontological imagination," the realm of dream and soul, maintains an independent level of reality, a "pre or beyond-human world soul." This realm often conveys "wisdom and insights that exceed ours," Keating writes, and therefore provides us with tools to realize "new forms of resistance," and alternative "visions of potential futures." This micro-manifesto for social change continues to draw from Anzaldúa's work, proposing that as a foundation for accessing and effectuating the ontological imagination for social change, we need a sufficient metaphysics of "radical interconnectedness" and practices of spiritual-imaginal alignment.

Matthew Segall's "Imagining a Gaian Reality After the Virus" considers how the modern, metaphysical divide between humans and nature needs to be upturned if postcapitalist futures are to be realized. Bringing Marx into critical dialogue with contemporary ecological thought, Segall turns to Alfred North Whitehead's philosophy of organism. What Whitehead offers our Gaian futures is a departure from teleological determinism, a cosmological move into "relational creativity" and Gaian agency.

In "Becoming Metamorphic: Moving Towards a New Conception of Life," Barbara Karlsen develops a metaphysics of the body as the site of perpetual unfoldment, suggesting that the future human may actualize hitherto unprecedented degrees of creative agency and individuation through plasticity and ecological relationality.

In "Revisiting *Coming Home*," Sean Kelly concludes this issue of *Mutations* with an appropriate temporal exercise in this updated epilogue to his 2010 book (*Coming Home: The Birth and Transformation of the Planetary Era*). While many developments, as Kelly writes, have proven to detract from a substantive hopefulness that civilization will avoid the "Great Unraveling," as Joanna Macy describes it, the loss of hope can deepen into faith. Without any expectations of salvation or success, the mutational leap into what Kelly calls a "planetary wisdom culture" ceases to be prefigurative. It becomes lived, an affirmation in the present—a faith in the highest good, and a coming home to a living cosmos.

Whatever else the integral mutation might be—and it is the hope of the editors that in the following pages we will be that much closer to finding out—at the very least it involves the realization, thunderclap sudden or slow-blooming spring assured, that we are already entangled in that radiant body of time, and so our tomorrow is always shaped in mutuality. In the *sympoiesis*, the "making-with" of the spiritual present, the world asks for our participation.[30]

Notes

1   Bruno Latour and Peter Weibel, *Critical Zones: The Science and Politics of Landing on Earth* (MIT Press, 2020), 47.
2   See Charles Ray Doyle, Wolfgang Mieder, and Fred R. Shapiro, *The Dictionary of Modern Proverbs* (Yale UP, 2012).
3   Franco Bifo Berardi, *After the Future* (AK Press, 2011), 18.
4   *Ibid.*, 25.
5   *Ibid.*, 22.
6   See Oneohtrix Point Never album lyrics:https://genius.com/Oneohtrix-point-never-cross-talk-ii-lyrics [last accessed Sept. 23, 2021}
7   Andreas Malm, *The Progress of This Storm: Nature and Society in a Warming World* (Verso, 2018), 5.
8   Ibid.
9   Justin Brice Guariglia, "WE ARE THE ASTEROID III" https://ybca.org/event/we-are-the-asteroid-iii/(Last Accessed September 23, 2021)
10 *Ibid.*
11 Marshall McLuhan, *Understanding Media: The Extensions of Man* (Signet Books, 1964), 27.
12 *Ibid.*
13 See Yanis Varoufakis, "Something remarkable has just happened this August." https://www.yanisvaroufakis.eu/2020/08/21/something-re-markable-just-happened-this-august-how-the-pandemic-has-sped-up-the-passage-to-postcapitalism-lannan-institute-virtual-talk/ [Last Accessed Sept 23, 2021]
14 Sean Kelly, *Becoming Gaia: On the Threshold of Planetary Initiation* (Integral Imprint, 2021), 29.
15 Marshall McLuhan, *The Medium is the Massage: An Inventory of Effects* (Bantam, 1967).
16 William Irwin Thompson, *Gaia: A Way of Knowing* (Lindisfarne Press, 1987), 212.
17 From *Asien lächelt anders* by Jean Gebser, translated excerpt by Aaron Cheak. See "Rendering Darkness and Light Present." http://www.aaroncheak.com/darkness-and-light [Last accessed September 23, 2021]
18 James Gallagher, "More than half your body is not human." https://www.bbc.com/news/health-43674270 [Last accessed September 23, 2021]
19 Arkady Martine, *A Memory Called Empire* (Tor, 2019), 235.
20 Timothy Morton, *All Art is Ecological* (Penguin Books, 2021), 104.
21 "Mutational urgency," is not doing something now or hurrying up to address a crisis. It is closer to the urgency of the artist who may feel

their creativity has possessed them—a creative urgency, a poeisis, of what is latent and wishes to be realized and the artist or maker who is fulfilled in the making.

22 Kim Stanley Robinson, https://www.newyorker.com/culture/annals-of-inquiry/the-coronavirus-and-our-future [Last accessed September 23, 2021]

23 Donna Haraway, "2016 Anthropocene Consortium Series: Donna Haraway" https://www.youtube.com/watch?v=fWQ2JYFwJWU [Last accessed Sept. 23, 2021]

24 Franco Bifo Berardi, *Futurability: The Age of Impotence and the Horizon of Possibility* (Verso, 2017) 13, 20.

25 Jean Gebser, *The Ever-Present Origin* (Ohio UP, 1985), 7.

26 Bruce Clarke, *Gaian Systems: Lynn Margulis, Cybernetics, and the End of the Anthropocene* (University of Minnesota Press, 2019), 208.

27 See Debashish Banerji, 2015 "Individuation, Cosmogenesis and Technology: Sri Aurobindo and Gilbert Simondon." *Integral Review* 11. 1 (February): 65–79.

28 William Gibson, "Technology, Science Fiction & the Apocalypse," 25th Anniversary Chicago Humanities Festival (lecture, November 6, 2014) https://www.youtube.com/watch?v=4dlvle5YBv4 (Date of Access: Sept. 23 2021)

29 Debashish Banerji, "Become a Silence that Calls in the Future," Cohering the Radical Present (class lecture, Nura Learning, November 11, 2020).

30 Donna Haraway, *Staying with the Trouble: Making Kin in the Chthulucene* (Duke UP, 2016).

Approaching the Origin:
The Diaphanous Body and
Classical Chinese Medicine

PERHAPS THE MOST OFT-REPEATED TALE from one of China's greatest literary and religious texts is a brief passage wherein:

Once Zhuang Zhou dreamed he was a butterfly, a butterfly flitting and fluttering around, happy with himself and doing as he pleased. Suddenly he woke up and there he was solid and unmistakable Zhuang Zhou. But he didn't know if he were Zhuang Zhou who had dreamed he was a butterfly, or a butterfly dreaming he was Zhuang Zhou. Between Zhuang Zhou and a butterfly there must be some distinction. This is called the Transformation of Things.[1]

In my practice of Chinese medicine, I have had many such experiences, not the least of which was, in a lightning-like flash, finding my own experience of the "Transformation of Things" reflected back to me in the work of cultural philosopher Jean Gebser. And, indeed, finding Gebser's own experience very reminiscent of my own.

I have pondered this question: am I trying to show the aperspectival aspects already nascently present within Chinese medicine? Or, am I trying to explain how Chinese medicine concepts can be transformed when looking through an aperspectival lens?

The answer lies in the "how" of my approach. Shen-Hammer pulse diagnosis, the core of my work, is in essence, a method that allows one to perceive all aspects of a human being's physiology in its most immediate and enduring manifestations—from gross physical bio-medical processes through the very spiritual expression of the intensification of becoming, and the evolution of being. After feeling thousands of pulses, and learning how to listen and relate with all aspects of my being, I sought a treatment model that could reflect the incredible depth and wholeness that I could perceive at my fingertips. And I found this same depth available in the Six Conformations as elaborated first in *Su Wen* Chapter 6, and more fully in the "Great Treatise" comprising Chapters 66–74 of the *Su Wen*. These concepts are the theoretical template upon which all possible manifestations of change and interaction are predicated, and form the basis for the entirely practical *Shang Han Za Bing Lun*, a text that sinologist and scholar-physician Heiner Fruehauf has described as marking "the first time that certain symptoms and pulses lead to diagnosis, which leads directly to a specific treatment-the dream of every Chinese medicine practitioner."[2]

This necessitated further inquiry into the classical texts that form the foundational basis of the Shang Han Lun. To my delight, I found those fundamental texts to be more inclusive of the entire corpus of the Han dynasty canon, especially those texts dealing with nature, consciousness, and inner cultivation. Even deeper in history, I found echoes of the basic human orientation to reflect a process of identifying with and fostering a relationship to the constant ebb and flow of all phenomena: what is termed animism, but from a Gebserian perspective can leap to a new mode that he terms synaeresis, or the "four-dimensional diaphany; in this what is merely conceivable and comprehensible becomes transparent. Diaphany is based on synaeresis, on the eteological completion of systasis and system to an integral whole..."[3]

This also recalls *Zhuang* Zi, Chapter 4:

Make your will one! Don't listen with your ears, listen with your mind. No, Don't listen with your mind, listen with your spirit. Listening stops with the ears, the mind stops with recognition, but spirit is empty and waits for all things. The Way gathers in emptiness alone. Emptiness is the fasting of the mind.[4]

So what of this spirit? Or rather, the spiritual? What of this emptiness? "The phenomenon releasing origin is spiritual, and with each consciousness mutation it becomes more realizable by man... the shining through (diaphaneity or transparency) is the form of appearance (epiphany) of the spiritual."[5] The emptiness described in the passage is not a void; it is a state of potential, and the very ground from which manifestation arises.

I note the similarity of the *Zhuang Zi* to a passage from *Su Wen* Chapter 26:

The spirit! Ah, the spirit! The ears do not hear it. When the physician's eyes are clear, his heart is open and his mind goes ahead. He alone apprehends [it as if it were] clearly perceivable. But the mouth cannot speak [of it]. Everyone looks, but he alone sees. If one approaches it, it seems obscure [but to him] alone it is obvious [as if it were] clearly displayed. As if the wind had blown away clouds, hence one speaks of spirit.[6]

In a flash, I, at a certain point, suddenly began to perceive, in a spherical expression, the state of those in my care. All the slings and arrows of outrageous fortune became palpable. Each patient began to look like a world unto herself, with all of the insults, and resources viscerally available to my consciousness. Visually, tactilely, cognitively, and presently, I beheld everyone as situated and embodied in a field of vast dimensions in which all things related. Acupuncture points became less textbook locations and became whole worlds of texture and structure imbued with wakeful presence. This experience accords with Gebser's definition of consciousness as "neither knowledge nor conscience...but in the broadest sense as wakeful presence."[7] Thus, embedded consciousness describes organisms within a relational field. It is a field not of inter-connected points but of interwoven lines: not a map, but a world. This recalls Gebser's assertion that:

the sphere is the expression of the aperspectival world. Aperspectivity is the "verition" the "awaring in truth" of the whole and consequently of its spiritual manifestation, the diaphainon, inasmuch as the whole is perceptible only as transparency wherein origin, also containing the entire future, is time-free present. To attain this consciously, without abandoning the earlier consciousness structures, is to overcome rationality in favor of arationality, and to break forth from mentality into diaphaneity.[8]

What followed from experiences such as this was also a new orientation to time. I had already begun to reframe the concept of Qi as the felt-sense. In adopting this simple shift, I experienced the process of needling as a form of making contact with the felt-sense that would arise, generating bodily awareness in a new way. As a corollary, I also paid close attention to my own felt sense, and then could perceive in my own body the awareness that the patient also experienced. I was already accustomed to deploying intense concentration in order to feel and differentiate the sensations in the pulse, taken in 28 positions and up to 8 depths on the radial arteries of both wrists. In order to feel the subtleties of communication that are available to perception, I also had to undergo a shift in my own perception of time. Because it is possible to feel pulse qualities that may point to an event that occurred many years previously, it was as if millimeters of space became filled with years of time, and within a single position I could feel, as a bare kinesthetic sensation different temporal strata in the patient's life experience. As an example, I once felt a series of sensations as I applied pressure to the wrist, that immediately informed me of the entire etiology of the onset of juvenile diabetes 20 or so years prior to the first visit with this patient—a febrile disease, a near-death experience from drowning at age 3, the death of a grandfather immediately at the time of the patient's birth, and then even deeper, the very effects of the damage to the pancreas that is associated with Type-1 diabetes. Likewise, the sensations that I feel in the pulse will be replicated in the channels and tissues of the body associated with the systems affected. In this case, when I found the acupuncture point through palpation, I also felt similar sensations at the tip of the needle, and I perceived an image of a dense mass of small, bulbous capsules and the words "islets of langerhans" came into my mind. After the treatment, I looked up this term, and of course found the image that I had seen. The patient's need for insulin injections began to lessen. The body had become transparent, and time itself expanded and contracted simultaneously in a moment.

From that point forward, I began to conceive of many of the

terms in Chinese medicine as expressions of time intersecting with human physiology. Some human functions are expressions of a diurnal cycle—such as what is termed organ Qi. Some functions are expressions of cycles of human maturation that unfold in 7- or 8-year increments—this is termed essence. Still others move at the rate of 15 inches a second (the speed at which blood exits the heart). Likewise, the many variegated channel systems elaborated by the early Chinese medical texts are also expressions of these same time-signatures. So, the main channels correspond to all aspects of human function that regulate diurnal processes, while the 8 Extraordinary vessels embody the 7 or 8 year cycles of essence. Yet these can all be employed together, and thus provide the bodily awareness with a means of joining these expressions into a total moment that essentially mends or restructures—renders immediately available to perception—multiple streams of duration, and trails of manifestation.

Several fundamental intensifications are necessary to, in verity, perceive in this manner. The first, and most pressing in our time, is to break through any dualistic, positivist, materialist focus. In Chinese medicine this means recognizing simultaneously the relationship between form and function in human physiology, to leap beyond pattern recognition and into the observation of relationships of things as they are in any given individual. Unfortunately the development of Chinese medicine in the modern era has not been free of this materialist, and pathology-oriented paradigm. Yet, "If we do not risk upsetting some persons and things, and indicate the inadequacy of systems with their categorical rigidities, we will not be able to approach the new world reality."[9]

The second is to recognize embodied cognition, in which one perceives all of the variegated functions actively constructing the lived-experience as nothing other than awareness, or wakeful presence. The principal avenues for this expression are recovering a felt-sense of the body, and regarding every physiological function and every pathological symptom as a message unfolding from, as the ancients might phrase it, Heaven. This simple shift accords with Gebser's treatment of creativity as an originary phenomenon, and naturally calls to mind the words famously attributed to the Tang Dynasty medical sage Sun Simiao (581–682): "Medicine is Change," or more interpretively to know medicine is tantamount to knowing Yi Jing science.

Gebser, of course, likewise appeals to the Yi Jing in his discussion of creativity. Two noteworthy aspects to his assessment exist. First, Gebser emphasizes the role of the incipient state: "we have quoted these lines since they can suggest to a thoughtful person how important it is to recognize the inceptual or germinal situations."[10] The term that is being translated here is Ji (幾) which is cognate with a technical term in the practice of Chinese medicine (機). In Chinese medicine the term appears in the first chapter of the *Ling Shu*—the most significant acupuncture text. The term also figures prominently in the related fields of alchemy and meditation (Bensky and Chace). We shall return to this notion later in the chapter.

Gebser's second astonishing insight, in his chapter devoted to creativity, is his recognition that the very antiquity of the names applied to the trigrams upon which the Yi Jing is based, and the etymology associated with the terms, suggests their origin in deeper, more archaic strata. Scholar Julie Lee Wei, in her 2005 Sino-Platonic Papers publication, convincingly demonstrates that the names of the trigrams correspond to the oldest forms of Old Sinitic, and are actually clear cognates of terms from Indo-European.[11] For example, *Zhen* corresponds to the Indo-European root for Old English *thunor* and modern *thunder*.[12] This minor point in Gebser's discussion underscores a significant presence within the literature of Chinese medicine and philosophy, of a more archaic, oral transmission. One term that I employ to describe this transmission is animism—or more pointedly, diasporanimism.

Animism is not to be confused with the notion of "primitive religion," an idea which Gebser himself interrogates according to his structural model.[13] Following reconsiderations of exactly what animism means, (such as those of Hallowell, Ingold, Bird-David, Martin, Willerslev, Nelson, and Kohn) I perceive, within the purview of Chinese medicine, a quality of movement and investigation that sees all spiritual health and well-being firmly ensconced in relationships with the natural and spiritual dimensions of the world, and sees human beings as participating in this great mystery internally and externally since time immemorial. That is, at the very roots of the history, cosmology, and philosophy underlying Chinese medicine there is a substrate of animistic consciousness. "To elaborate: life in the animic ontology is not an emanation but a generation of being, in a world that is not pre-ordained but incipient, forever on the verge of the actual."[14] And further,

...there is no inside or outside, and no boundary separating the two domains. Rather there is a trail of movement or growth. Every such trail traces a relation. But the relation is not between one thing and another—between the organism "here" and the environment "there." It is rather a trail along which life is lived: one strand in a tissue of trails that together make up the texture of the lifeworld. That texture is what I mean when I speak of organisms being constituted within a relational field. It is a field not of inter-connected points but of interwoven lines, not a network but a meshwork.

Nevertheless the depiction of the single line is of course a simplification. For the lives of organisms generally extend along not one but multiple trails, branching out from a source. We should imagine the organism, then, not as a self-contained object like a ball that can propel itself from place to place, but as an ever ramifying web of lines of growth. The philosophers Gilles Deleuze and Félix Guattari (1983) famously likened this web to a rhizome, though I prefer the image of the fungal mycelium.[15]

While I also love Deleuze and Guattari's characterization of the rhizome, and can appreciate the image of the mycelium (the unseen structure that produces fungal fruiting bodies as its manifestation in the visible), an equally apt characterization of the relational ontology is embodied in the myriad pathways of animation (the entire channel system) described by Chinese medicine, and their manifestation in the Opening, Pivoting, and Closing of Yin and Yang. That is, the very energetic structure that constitutes the body in Chinese medicine, comprised if both form and function, matter and energy is also rhizomic in its intricacy, and autopoeitic in manifestation.

Likewise, within the contiguous junctions of all these pathways one also sees the relational, rhizomic unfolding of consciousness itself. The Channel System in its entirety, and the patterns of organization upon which these are modeled, is an example of the three-dimensional incarnation of consciousness and animation itself as is the world in which this animation unfolds. Contained within this three-dimensional embodiment, though, we may also uncover the seeds of time-freedom as fourth-dimensionality. "Anyone able to realize and thus concretize the three previously basic temporal forms already consciously stands in four-dimensionality."[16]

In order to fully perceive the "one truth" of Three Yin and Three Yang, one must allow awareness to flower in concert with the multi-dimensional vastness of its very expression and manifestation. That means that if we would truly comprehend this truth, then our own awareness must be flowing with 順 *shun* the very self-same unfolding that informs the process of becoming. And if we do not confine this only to its magical expression as power, or its psychic and vitalist strains, but instead strive towards the intensificiation necessary to the realization of an aperspectival, integral consciousness, then it is the very unfolding of states of consciousness as Gebser describes it that can be posited as the true potential that such an unfolding process that comprises the flow we must fully embody into a state of true a-spatial and a-temporal freedom.

This image returns us anew to the phenomenological depth of the ancient Chinese perspective, especially as it describes a situated, embodied consciousness. Phenomenological philosopher Merleau-Ponty employs the term *Umwelt* (a term borrowed from von Uexküll) to describe embedded perception. Focusing on the relationship between consciousness and awareness also recalls the insistence of Dr. Leon Hammer that, as clinicians we bear two major charges: to seek to know how the patient, as an individual, experiences the world, and secondly that our success is measured in the degree to which we offer something other than the typical response. In light of the phenomenological perspective outlined here however, we might consider that each individual constitutes a world in her own right.

And that, as the formulas of the *Shang Han Lun* are based on the very structural principles through which the worlds manifest, that each iteration of these formulae constitute equally a world-making in progress. And thus, the assimilation of these stimuli into the very Flesh (the inter-subjective as Merleau-Ponty describes it, but also literally through metabolism) is necessarily to participate in something other than the typical response. There is only one pathology in all of Chinese medicine, and that is flowing against (逆 Ni) the flow of the numinous. Yet in taking up Gebser's call, we might also describe this flow as awakening consciousness:

It is the task of this work to serve towards the liberation which can be completed only via the awakening consciousness of the spiritual. And, we might add, it is not a question of "being right," but of being true. This is a greater demand than the mentally-conditioned desire to be right which is, moreover, patriarchal and egocentric.[17]

Allopathic, meaning opposition, does not flow with but rather against, and all-too-often represents the typical response to pathology, and in our times is deeply constrained by mental-rational constructs. Since these chinese medicine modalities embody the establishment of flow, then, instead they promote the resonance of the affected conformation with its natural physiological state, and participate in the creation of an entirely new world for each and every patient: and this is a world that is itself alive, animated, embodied and potentially integral.

Further elaboration of the insights of Merleau-Ponty occurs in the work of Francisco Varela and extends our reach into the realm of cognitive science, consciousness studies, and a growing call towards a first-person science that recognizes subjectivity. In *Dragon Rises, Red Bird Flies*, Dr. Hammer asserts that in the Chinese medicine model it is impossible to exclude the role of the healer in the healing process, while at the same time elaborating that the final and ineluctable step in any healing venture must be taken by that patient herself. This is to articulate precisely the thrust of a first-person science. The drive to include the subjective in our estimation of reality and consciousness is likewise a move that demonstrates just how vital the earliest articulation of Chinese medicine theory can be in explaining consciousness. But even more importantly it also paves the way for a therapeutics based upon a congenial partnership between function and form, consciousness and the body, and Yang and Yin. It also admits of "the disruption of the merely systematic, the incursion of dynamics, (and) the recognition of energy..."[18] And, in the words of my teacher Leon Hammer: "If we experience energy as a reality, we must acknowledge it in its totality."[19]

As a neuroscientist and philosopher, Varela's work also directs our inquiry into the net-like quality of consciousness itself, which is reflected in the very structures of the nervous system. In *The Embodied Mind,* Varela draws upon the phenomenological inquiry of Merleau-Ponty to describe Enaction, or embodied cognition. Quoting from Merleau-Ponty's early writings, he describes how "the properties of the object and the intentions of the subject...are not only intermingled; they also constitute a new whole."[20] The premise of the enactive approach is that there is no perceiver-independent world, but instead that the entire sensorimotor and perceptual faculty is enacted from within a framework of immersion in the constantly evolving interaction between the environment, the stimuli, and the terrain of embodied consciousness. In short, "Sensory and motor processes, perception and action, are fundamentally inseparable in lived cognition."[21] This invites a further discussion on the very categories within which the union of perception and action are enacted. "The basic level of categorization, thus, appears to be the point at which cognition and environment become simultaneously enacted... Form and function, normally investigated as opposing properties, are aspects of the same process, and organisms are highly sensitive to their coordination."[22]

On an even more material level, the concept of neuronal networks describes the means by which such simultaneity is processed on a cellular level. In *The Dao of Neuroscience,* the example of Indra's Net is employed to model the interaction of neural networks. Indra's Net is an image of an infinite interlocking network extending in all directions, and in which at each intersection there is an embedded jewel. And every jewel within this net, reflects every other jewel in the entire web. The concept of neuronal networks is based upon describing the interactions of neurons, as a network of simple structures, in the same manner. The significance of the model suggests that "rather than a linear chain in which one cause sets one effect in motion, a net of cause-and-effect interrelationships among many things forms, to bring about many effects. At a higher level of understanding, all events of reality are interconnected in a web, interdependent and co-created by each other. Through this holistic pattern, reality as we know it comes to be, and similarly brain structures and functions come to be as well."[23] Just as cognition is an autopoietic function, the very physical structure of the neuronal networks is also—in terms of both its function and its form, its maintenance and generation—autopoietic.

In essence, the confluence of all these models across many disciplines and modes of experience, simply recapitulates the premise that the Six Conformations model describes a comprehensive interpretation of the interaction of Yin and Yang, through the processes of release and return, that describes how entire worlds are constructed from the most cosmological level to the most minute neuronal organization. Thus, we approach the one truth attested to in SW 6.

Within *Su Wen* Chapter Six [SW 6] (The Treatise on Release and Return of Yin and Yang, trans. Givens), we perceive that the six transformations of the conformations include the entire phenomenological representation of what it means to live as a human being at the intersection of Heaven and Earth. For Qi Bo responds to Huang Di saying:

As for Yin and Yang, their numbers can reach ten; extended they can reach one hundred; extended further still, they can reach ten thousand; the vastness of the ten thousand is beyond counting, however their truth is One.

Within this one truth is found a complete description of how the mandate of Heaven is embodied into the receptive material realm of Yin. "Now, in the operations of change and transformation, heaven hangs the images, while the earth completes the physical appearances.[24] Ultimately, the one truth is an expression of Yin and Yang itself. As the Nei Ye, the earliest text of meditation in the Chinese tradition, advises, one must "hold fast to the One." The Six Conformations represent a complete picture of the relationship between the microcosm and macrocosm that is the root of Classical Chinese Medicine. But to elevate this One from its foundation in a magical state of unity alone, we must recognize that the notion of the void is not at all devoid of potential. It is not a description of the inert, inactive state of quiescence in its magical or archaic form: it is itself the ever-present Origin that is creative and luminous.

At the origins of Chinese herbal medicine, the Warring States period *Shang Han Lun* of Zhang Zhong Jing employs the six expressions of Yin and Yang as a means of organizing a treatise on how to counteract pernicious influences on human physiology.

In our definition of human physiology, from the classical perspective, we must accept the absolute integrity of body and mind. All aspects of human experience are non-dual in nature; awareness and experience (which includes the body itself) are not two, they are one. There has been considerable debate in modern times, both in Asia and the West, regarding the meaning of the term 神 *Shen*, varying in significant degrees from more positivist perspectives to relatively more immaterial or cosmologically significant views. None of these are to be discounted if we are to fully comprehend the meaning of the ineffable mystery that underlies all of human existence. Within this mystery, arising out of a state of pure potential that exists before the alternation of Yin and Yang grinding together to generate all processes of life, the *Nei Jing* describes 神 *Shen* as that state of potential itself. Within the breathing of the cosmos, it is the 神明 *Shenming* that represents the organizing principle that emerges as light, and energy, to suffuse life and matter. "The special quality of 神明 *shenming* is seen to be a basic prerequisite for all life processes and, as such, it is seen to contain the original template upon which life originally forms itself."[25]

Underlying the classical model, and evident in the very archi-tecture of the formulas themselves, is this understanding of normal human physiology, and how to restore it in the event of injurious influences. Within the Yang Realm, Shaoyang occupies the pivot, Taiyang is the Open state, and Yangming Closes the Yang realm so that it can enter Yin. Within the Yin realm, Shaoyin is the pivot, Tai-yin is the Open state, and Jueyin Closes so that Yin can support the emergence of Yang. Just as Yin represents form, and Yang represents function, Yin is the material realm, and Yang is the immaterial. But once again, we must always recall that the truth of these variable states or qualities of Yang are truthfully one.

Another set of relationships informs the interaction of the Six conformations, and actually provides the key to their co-arising. Each is joined in a Yin/Yang pair that is described in terms of its Manifestation (Biao), its Root or core energetic function (Ben), and its Center (Zhong Qi). Each pair describes a set of functions that provide balance to all physiological activities, and also form the basis for the science of *Wu Yun Liu Qi (五 運 六 氣),* or the Five Periods and Six Qi, a set of interactions "assumed to exist between climate and a broad range of natural phenomena, including human health and illness."[26] See the table *(facing page).*

In their entirety, these functions differentiate Yin and Yang into a set of relationships that describe the expansive and contractive forces comprising the very breathing of the cosmos, and as such con-form to the pattern whereby everything comes into being from an ultimately creative ground-of-being. Likewise, the pattern of three yang and three yin can describe the course of human development both physically and spiritually, proceeding from birth-to-death, an annual cycle, in which both seasons and associated astrological phenomena can be mapped, and a diurnal cycle, in which midnight is the nadir and noon is its apex.

Tracing a lifetime across a circle, just as the Sun seems to trace a circle through the sky, under the earth, and rising anew in the East, one sees that it is the vital spark of Yang that gives rise to life, Yang that allows the motion of inspiration and exhalation, the rising

Conformation/role	Biao	Ben	Zhong Qi
Shaoyang-Pivot	Gallbladder/ Triple Burner	Ministerial Fire	Jueyin
Taiyang- Open	Urinary Bladder/ Small Intestine	Cold	Shaoyin
Yangming-Closing	Stomach/ Large Intestine	Dryness	Taiyin
Shaoyin- Pivot	Kidney/Heart	Imperial Fire	Taiyang
Taiyin- Open	Spleen/Lung	Dampness	Yangming
Jueyin- Closing	Liver/Pericardium	Wind/Wood	Shaoyang

of Wood in the East, and the descending of Metal in the West, and ultimately *moves* one inevitably to return to a state of quiescent immersion in the Water that will extinguish the spark, and free the soul for release into the One. Thus, when one looks into the mystery of this cycle, all manifestations of evolution and becoming rely on the Yang being "commanded to the Yin." Or, as Wang Bing comments, "Yang is the guiding factor in the dynamics of Yin and Yang."

This is also described in *Su Wen* Chapter 6:

Heaven covers [the myriad beings]. The Earth carries [them]. When the myriad beings just come to life, before they emerge from the earth, [this is called the location of Yin] this is called the Yin in the Yin. When they emerge from the earth, then this is called Yang in the Yin. Yang provides [the myriad beings] with proper Qi; Yin Qi rules them. Hence they come to life in the Spring; they grow through Summer, they are collected through Autumn; they are stored away through Winter.[27]

What has been described thus far, especially as it is based on a recurring and cyclical pattern of seasons can be illustrated by a circle. As soon as we posit, however, the inter-relationships between the different stages as they occur, we transcend the circle and approach the simultaneity and rhizomic interweaving of function that describes a truly autopoietic system. For at any given time, all of the functions of the organism are occurring.

In the *Shang Han Lun*, representative statements of the signs and symptoms open each chapter, and when we perceive the underlying functions that those symptoms describe, then we perceive its role in the bodymind. In the Shaoyin chapter, for example, the chief symptom is somnolence. Later in the same chapter, a pattern of insomnia is presented. Both somnolence and insomnia describe a change in the state of consciousness; indeed, the most basic and simple alteration of consciousness that one experiences every day. Yet as soon as we perceive this pattern, then we have achieved a transparent seeing that recalls Gebser's glowing approbation of Paul Klee's statement: "I more and more see behind, or better through things."[28] We may extend this single pattern to also imply that the Yang impulse towards movement into the future is submerged in the stasis of immersion in the Yin: one may be sleep-walking through life, or else unable to initiate the downward introjection of consciousness necessary to rest, and restore the basic energy of life. Death itself is a consequence of the complete expiration and loss of functional contact in this realm: the total separation of Yin and Yang.

This further illustrates the relationship between the Center (zhong qi) and the Manifestation (Biao). In this case, the quality of our basic orientation to existence is mediated at the periphery by the system Taiyang: the interface of our body with its environment. Another way that this can be described is as the relationship between the autonomic nervous system and the peripheral nervous system, or as the two poles of interaction between the body-condition as a whole (the internal milieu), and its response to insults in the form of stress. Another way to say the same thing is to reiterate that "cognition and environment become simultaneously enacted... Form and function, normally investigated as opposing properties, are aspects of the same process, and organisms are highly sensitive to their coordination."[29] All of the interactions of the different conformations can be approached in a similar manner and when viewed in this manner bring us close to a "method" which in Gebser's terms would be called systasis. "Systasis is the conjoining or fitting together of parts into integrality..." and he cautions us to recognize that it is not a causal system, but rather "both process and effect."[30]

It is impossible to ever truly isolate physical from non-physical parts from the whole. Thus, if we regard symptoms as both process and effect, then something as simple as a muscle tension, is as much an indication of one's whole-being-in-the-world as is the fear of the great unknown, or death. With that caveat in mind, however, we will examine the role of the Six Conformations in expressing the totality of the psychic and emotional life.

In Shaoyin/Water, we face the very exigencies of existence. Interchangeably, our existence is necessarily embodied in Taiyin/Earth. In Jueyin/Yin-Wood, we assert our being as other-than and unique. In Shaoyang/Yang-Wood, this manifests in the world, through all of the activities of metabolism. In Taiyang/Fire/South, this activity manifests in the full expression and positive assertion of our being, and we are capable of communicating this in our interactions with the world. In Yangming/Metal, we introject and intensify our being as autonomous agents capable of metanoia, and through constantly engaged rites-of-passage re-affirm and return to constantly changing and evolving expressions of our being in Shaoyin/Water anew.

Since all of these conformations likewise interface with everyaspect of physiology, when one suffers inhibition or excessive stimulation of any of the physiological functions, then symptoms result- providing a message about how the unfolding of process is interrupted. Such messages are indeed out of time. The etiology of a given condition may have its alpha-state at birth (often in the form of birth trauma for example), but only produces symptoms when the tipping point of life circumstance is reached in an omega-state. However, the body itself retains the stamp of this initial insult in a space beyond the spatial, and in a time beyond the temporal, even as simultaneously it auto-poeitically reorients its homesotatic intelligence to account for this influence.

The nature of the symptoms, can be understood in terms of the precise stage in which the stress capitalizes upon a vulnerability. So for example, if one is inhibited in the No-stage of development (the Wood/Jueyin sphere) wherein the negative assertion of being is met with repression and humiliation, then there will be an inhibition of the capacity for self-determination and the drive towards directed action in moving towards a goal. As Gebser articulates, "what is decisive for us is to know in any given instance where and how to act passively or actively, where and how to make things happen or let things happen to us."[31] This knowledge is itself predicated upon the Yang/active or Yin/passive engagement with life. The freedom to say this existential "No!" is itself necessary in order to know when to advance and when to retreat. The capacity for movement and action is expressed physically through a workable, supple movement in the interaction of the musculo-skeletal system working in conjunction with the peripheral nervous system. Likewise, in governing the dilation and constriction of blood vessels we can see how the entirety of the body's capacity for the circulation of blood is also a function of Yin and Yang as expressed through the autonomic nervous system. In other words, one is either in a state of sympathetic hyperarousal (fight or flight) or parasympathetic dominance (rest and digest). In terms of the emotional sphere, this could present as a state of hyper-vigilant anxiety and tension, or the withdrawal represented by depression that will still carry the imprint of agitation derived from an impotence to take action. With a completely overwhelming and destabilizing influence, psychosis with catatonic features will ensue. To address such a situation, it is necessary to restore assertion and circulation within the Wood or Jueyin sphere. But we must also be cognizant that, if this is both "process and effect" simultaneously, then our attention will likewise be drawn to the rising Wood/Jueyin's counterpart found in the introspective, downward pull of Metal/Yangming. In other words, when the free flow is restored to function, it must be communicated in image and narrative in the realm of Fire, so that the metanoia of Metal/Yangming introspection can also be stimulated- a rite of passage that yields a new experience of one's right to exist, and a new expression of the essence of one's being that is experienced in the depths of our being within Water/Shaoyin. If all of these variegated expressions are seen, this is a synairesis, "an integral act of completion "encompassing all sides" and perceiving aperspectivally."[32] Or, as described in the *Nei Jing* passage quoted earlier, seeing as if the wind had blown away clouds, thus we speak of spirit.

Gebser is unequivocal in his statement that "the new mutation of consciousness, on the other hand, as a consequence of arationality, receives its decisive stamp from the manifest perceptual emergence of the spiritual."[33] And he goes further to suggest that "the grand and painful path of consciousness emergence, or, more appropriately, the unfolding and intensification of consciousness, manifests itself as an increasingly intense luminescence of the spiritual in man."[34]

These pathways can likewise be seen to conform to the same unfolding of Yin and Yang, in its magical unity, mythical expression as complementarity, and mental-rational differentiation. The Shaoyin, as water, and the very source itself represents Origin, the basis of all that we are, containing within it both the past and future of our being. The Jueyin, associated as it is with blood, describes the magical emergence of attempts to protect the self in the first blush of a striving to gain power over nature. The Shaoyang pivots into the Taiyang as man begins to express mythical consciousness through word, image, and symbol, finally establishing the greatest distanciation in Yangming where the self became subject to adequate intensificiation to drive the final leap into the mutation of the Integral. Expressing as it does the ever-present Origin, the unfathomable Shen 神 resides in Shaoyin and takes expression in the core of our being as the fundamental, inseparable axis of Fire and Water, now seen through with limpid perspicacity. It is the luminescence of the spiritual that can actually shine forth as Shenming 神明, described earlier as the very principle through which life shines forth in the bodymind. And this is not housed anywhere, but expresses itself only through the whole.

To perceive this principle, we are counseled to seek the dynamic Ji 機 in its holistic, incipient state, to observe its emergence in the breathing of the cosmos as it emerges and is matched by the interplay of Yin and Yang in the microcosm. In order to perceive anything in its incipient state however, one must cultivate a quality of attention and focus. I follow Dr. Leslie Allan Combs in affirming that "consciousness is essentially a subjective presence."[35] I also maintain that the experience of integral consciousness and diaphaneity is essentially a non-dual mode, and as such can be seen to have a great deal in common with non-dual awareness as understood in dzog-chen, and in the early Daoist texts, amongst others. One of the principle avenues to developing this type of awareness begins with meditation on the breath, and leads to the perception of the immediate, luminous, infinitely creative and auto-presencing manifestation of awareness. I have described this process in the Six Conformations, as an intensification of consciousness associated with the introjective gesture of the Yangming/Metal that returns one to wholeness, and renews the vital circulation.

The earliest epigraphical evidence for this type of inner cultivation has been unearthed in the form of a carving on what is known as the Duodecagonal Jade Tablet Inscription on the Circulation of Qi:

To Circulate Qi,
Swallow it so that it will accumulate.
As it accumulates, it will expand.
As it expands it will descend.
As it descends it will stabilize.
As it stabilizes it will consolidate.
As it consolidates it will sprout.
As it sprouts it will grow.
As it grows it will return.
As it returns it will merge with Heaven.
The heavenly impulses are revealed in the rising of qi.
The earthly impulses are revealed in the descending of qi.
Go along with this and you will live.
Go against it and you will die.

In closing, the Six Conformations, as they describe this expansion and contraction, rising and descending, provide access to lived, embodied experience. The closer one attends to somatic experience the more one perceives the creative interplay of the bodymind and the lifeworld. With perception of the diaphanous body, pleni-potentiality is not far away. Closer! Closer! Vast! Vast! The world of the multivalent arising is entered through the door of the breath. Breath, indeed, is the Yin/Yang expression of the universe unfolding. Breath carries sound. Sound waves move like waves of vibration. Vibrations illuminate the fecund darkness of all potentials, yielding a transparency: diaphaneity. The Breath feels like light sounds: the Origin is ever-present.

Notes

1   Burton Watson, *The Complete Works of Zhuangzi* (Columbia UP, 2013), 18.
2   Heiner Fruehauf, *32 Classical Chinese Medicine: An Introduction to the Foundational Concepts and Political Circumstance of an Ancient Science* (Hai Shan Press, 2007), 32.
3   Jean Gebser, *Ever-Present Origin* (Ohio UP, 1985), 334.
4   Watson, *Zhuangzi* 25.
5   Gebser, *EPO*, 542.
6   Paul Unschuld, *Huangdi Nei Jing Su Wen* (University of California Press, 2003), 445.
7   Gebser, *EPO*, 42.
8   *Ibid.*, 412.
9   *Ibid.*, 308.
10 *Ibid.*, 314.
11 Available at https://www.sino-platonic.org/
12 *Ibid.*
13 Gebser, *EPO*, 270.
14 Tim Ingold, "Rethinking the Animate, Re-Animating Thought," *Ethnos* 71.1 (2006): 9–20.
15 Tim Ingold, "Two Reflections on Ecological Knowledge," 302–6, in *Nature Knowledge: Ethnoscience, Cognition, Identity*, edited by G. Sanga & G. Ortalli, (Berghahn, 2003).
16 Gebser, *EPO*, 356.
17 *Ibid.*, 361.
18 *Ibid.*, 362.
19 Leon Hammer, *Dragon Rises, Red Bird Flies* (Eastland Press, 2005), xxxvii.
20 Francisco Varela, Evan Thompson, and Eleanor Rosch, *The Embodied Mind* (MIT Press, 1996), 174.

21 *Ibid.*, 173.

22 *Ibid.*, 177.

23 Annellen Simpkins and C. Alexander Simpkins, *Dao of Neuroscience* (W.W. Norton, 2010), 26.

24 Unschuld, *Huangdi Nei Jing Su Wen*, 197.

25 Edward Neal, "Introduction to Neijing Acupuncture Part II: Clinical Theory," *The Journal of Chinese Medicine* 102 (2013): 20–31.

26 Unschuld, *Huangdi Nei Jing Su Wen*, 393.

27 *Ibid.*, 128–29.

28 Jean Gebser, *The Invisible Origin*, as translated by Theo Rottgers, "Jean Gebser The Invisible Origin: Evolution as a Supplementary Process," *Journal of Conscious Evolution* 1.1 (2018): 25.

29 Varela, *Embodied Mind*, 177.

30 Gebser, *EPO*, 310.

31 *Ibid.*, 138.

32 *Ibid.*, 312.

33 *Ibid.*, 541.

34 *Ibid.*, 542.

35 Allan Combs, *The Radiance of Being* (Paragon House, 2002), 257.

Climate Crisis, Karma, Compassion

IT ALREADY SURROUNDS US. It's in the air. It's in the weather, but it's not the weather. It's more than moisture, wind, heat, or a lack thereof. Much is known about it, yet it evades understanding, too immense to comprehend. Changing it can render the planet uninhabitable for so many species, including humans. It poses the existential emergency of mass extinction, but it bears a deceptively simple moniker, "climate." Climate change is not what it seems to be.

Climate is not just a statistical average of interlocking dynamics of temperature, wind, air pressure, humidity, and precipitation. A changing climate involves more than a shift in a long-term average pattern of atmospheric conditions. Climate change as a planetary system of dynamic, interconnected weather patterns is a part of a more complex whole, and not only in the sense that the global climate is connected to all the systems of water, land, air, and life on Earth. More than saying that climate change is about the whole Earth and not just the atmosphere, the point is that climate exceeds the limits of definitions articulated in the natural sciences, and that a wider field of inquiry is needed, one that includes socioeconomic, cultural, and existential dimensions of climate along with theories and observations from natural sciences. If we can figure out what climate change is, then we can better understand how best to respond to it.

What is it?

In the same way that an atmosphere can refer, on one hand, to a mood, and on the other hand, to a system of gases surrounding a planet, a climate has physical and sociocultural dimensions.

As part of a whole, Hulme describes climate change as a synecdoche that stands for 1) a modern social system, 2) an economic ideology, 3) a loss of nature, and 4) a new geological epoch.[1] For Hulme, that social system is best described by Ulrich Beck's analysis of the "risk society" of modernity, which is based on the management of hazards and uncertainties that society produces through its never-ending pursuit of progress and wealth.[2]

Hulme follows Naomi Klein in identifying capitalism as the economic ideology of climate change.[3] It is an ideology for which the accumulation of wealth for the few happens at the expense of the many, thus producing social and ecological disasters, which then become justification for the further deployment of capitalist tactics, producing yet further disasters in an accelerating loop of what Klein calls "disaster capitalism."[4] To be sure, liberalism and conservatism are both complicit in disaster capitalism. The liberal face of this ideology is the identity politics that incorporates people of diverse subject positions (races, sex, genders, abilities, etc.) to participate in the system, as if bringing more people closer to the wealthy top will eventuate in justice for the myriad beings at the disastrously impoverished bottom.

Along with the risk society and capitalist ideology, Hulme's definition of climate change also includes the end of nature, which has been a topic of increasingly frequent discussion among environmental thinkers, with notable contributions like Carolyn Merchant's classic ecofeminist text, *The Death of Nature*, and Bill McKibben's book on climate change, *The End of Nature*, which were first published in 1980 and 1989 respectively. Many recent explorations of this topic refer to Timothy Morton's theory of ecological criticism in his 2007 book *Ecology without Nature*. Climate change is part of the loss of the relatively regular, stable, ordered ground of nature, which is also a loss of ideas and fantasies of Nature as a big Other, whether friend or foe, sacred or profane. The regular patterns and ordered systems of nature have gradually become displaced as humans have extended their environmental impacts all around the planet, becoming an Earth-shaping force. The catastrophic loss of nature is thus entwined with a new geological epoch.

As modern humans began adding high amounts of carbon, plutonium, plastic, Styrofoam, and a wide assortment of artificial chemicals to Earth's crust, the geological epoch of the last 12,000 years (the Holocene) gave way to a new one that bares the indelible stamp of *Homo sapiens*, the Anthropocene. It is a controversial name, to be sure. It is not clear if this is indeed a new epoch or merely a boundary event between epochs. Furthermore, humans did not all participate equally in facilitating this geological transformation. Humans in WEIRD social locations (Western, Educated, Industrialized, Rich, and Democratic) are particularly responsible, yet that culpability and complicity is erased by the general humanity of *Anthropos*. The problem of nomenclature notwithstanding, the loss of nature marks the end of a natural Earth and the beginning of an Earth where the natural and the artificial have imploded. It is an Earth become artifact, "Eaarth," as McKibben puts it. In sum, along with a change in average atmospheric conditions, climate change also stands for the end of nature, a change in geological epochs, and a society that, for the sake of progress and wealth accumulation, is willing to risk massive destruction, death, and extinction.[5]

With its sociocultural and biophysical dimensions overlapping in cause-effect cycles that extend from humans through the land, life, air, and water of Earth, climate change can be understood as a change in *karma*—the Sanskrit word for "action," denoting a cause-effect principle discussed in Indian philosophies (e.g., Vedanta, Yoga, Jainism, and Buddhism). Karma includes all the cause-effect dynamics of all energy (psychological and physical) circulating on Earth and throughout the cosmos. Consider these remarks from the Tibetan Buddhist, Chögyam Trungpa Rinpoche:

All the processes that take place in the universe are dependent on the environmental situation of karma. It is rather like the atmosphere that the planet requires in order to function, in order for things to grow. When we talk about the karmic situation, we are speaking about the sense of individual relationship to the given situation, whatever it is. Any given situation is bounded by cause and effect, dependent on some cause and effect. [...] So, altogether when we discuss karma, we are discussing energy.[6]

Karma includes enlightened action, such as the activity of the Buddha, as well as the action of one caught in *samsara*—the cycle of confusion and suffering. The difference is duality. In the samsaric condition, karma is "energy that moves from here to there and then bounces back," which is "the definition of duality," more specifically, it is "duality in the sense of the neurosis of dualistic fixation."[7] Enlightened energy undoes the dualistic fixation through wisdom and compassion.

What is the cause of global warming? Is it globalization, industrialization, capitalism, technoscience, modernity, patriarchy, agriculture, or the so-called "Western" worldview? What if those are all symptoms, and the cause driving our cause-effect cycle of global warming is samsaric energy? What if there is a neurotic fixation that keeps human action in a state of confusion? What if too much carbon in the atmosphere is caused by too much dualism in our karma? Can compassion help us escape this crisis?

How Do We Respond?

It is difficult, to say the least, to articulate and respond to the challenges of discerning what should be done in a situation like this. If climate change overflows conventional definitions of climate and implicates humans within massively distributed cycles of karma, so too does it exceed the limits of the predominant approaches to ethics, which tend to follow along the lines of anthropocentrism, maintaining a rigid wall between humans and nonhumans while privileging the virtue and value of the former. The separation of humans and nonhumans is the dualistic fixation driving the climate crisis, so the old anthropocentrism won't work.

Unfortunately, instead of letting go of anthropocentric fantasies, it often feels much easier to simply reinvent them, as if a new and improved fantasy will get us out of the mess that we're in. For example, the idea of the Anthropocene prompts Clive Hamilton to propose a "new anthropocentrism," new insofar as it accords with "the arrival of a geological epoch in which humans now rival the great forces of nature."[8] Hamilton is ostensibly aware of critiques of anthropocentrism, but for him, "the Anthropocene arrives to blow them all away and instantiate humankind once and for all as the being at the center of the Earth. As each year passes, the chasm between human beings and every other creature only widens."[9] He says he is making a descriptive and not normative claim, as if humans simply are necessarily anthropocentric now, whether we like it or not, whether we think we should be or not. Normatively, he suggests that he would rather not have anthropocentrism, but unfortunately the constraints of the real world demand it. It is not unlike me saying that I would rather not have people get sick and die. If only we could be non-anthropocentric, embracing the intrinsic values of life forms and ecosystems instead of forcing all value to revolve around humans, but alas, our hands are tied. This is simply the way things are. We must be anthropocentric. The Anthropocene made us do it. The Anthropocene is forcing us humans (who exactly?) to be anthropocentric, instantiating us at Earth's center, opening up an unbridgeable gulf between us and nonhumans.

That is simply incorrect. Tim Morton has it right when he says, *"Anthropocene is the first fully antianthropocentric concept."*[10] Far from demonstrating a widening chasm between humans and nonhumans, climate change inextricably enmeshes human, geological, and biological actors. The arrival of the Anthropocene adds profound perforation, fuzziness, and ambiguity to the boundaries that distinguish humans from nonhumans. Impacting the chemistry of the atmosphere does not grant humans exceptional value and agency, and large-scale risk-taking should not be confused with a state of being in control or in charge. Nonhumans such as fossil fuels, carbon dioxide molecules, and the biosphere have a more central role in human decision-making than ever before. While some humans might set themselves up as a "rival" to great natural forces—capitalism vs. the climate—it is a hasty generalization to enroll all of humankind in this rivalry, and it is quite simply hubristic to think that the rivalry is little more than a fantasy. All humans eventually succumb to entropy and die. It is hard to maintain the idea that

Climate Crisis, Karma, Compassion   39

humankind has been instantiated at the center of the Earth, considering that human life depends heavily upon an atmosphere that would be stripped away by solar winds if not for the protection of a magnetic field, which is generated by the currents of the molten core at the *actual* center of the Earth.

Ecological emergencies have rendered anthropocentrism more untenable than ever by confronting humankind with its fragile yet inescapable interconnectedness with nonhumans. That interconnectedness is what Morton calls "the ecological thought," which "creeps over us to deliver a message of unbearable intimacy."[11] This "unbearable intimacy with others" brings the anthropocentric human back down to the humus of Earth in a "'humiliating' descent":

Ecology is the latest in a series of great humiliations of the human, humiliations that might even constitute the human as such (in its humility, at least, if any). From Copernicus through Marx, Darwin and Freud, we learn we are decentered beings, inhabiting a Universe of processes that happen whether we are aware of them or not, whether we name those processes "astrophysics," "economic relations," "the unconscious" or "evolution."[12]

The humiliation of the human has accompanied the rise of ecological emergencies that have put an end to the idea of a stable background called "Nature." The ecological thought is "ecology without Nature." Moreover, this thought is not based on a metaphysical theory but on the sheer coexistence of things. Ecological emergency just is this coexistence. We need a "coexistentialism" that affirms this unbearable intimacy.[13]

The world as the stage upon which humans act out a central role has ended, with the stage shattering into countless multiplicities of actors each clamoring for attention. It is only in and as solidarity with nonhumans that human beings can find themselves. It is only through the inhuman that humankind can grow forth. We can hear this idea expressed in an early (1872) piece by Friedrich Nietzsche, whose prescience surely foreshadowed the Anthropocene.

If we speak of *humanity*, it is on the basic assumption that it should be that which *separates* man from nature and is his mark of distinction. But in reality there is no separation: "natural" characteristics and those called specifically "human" have grown together inextricably. Man, in his highest, finest powers, is all nature and carries nature's uncanny character in himself. Those capacities of his which are terrible and are viewed as inhuman are perhaps, indeed, the fertile soil from which alone all humanity, in feelings, deeds and works, can grow forth.[14]

Letting that which is inhuman into our humanity might sound dangerous. It could seem like we cannot trust that the coexistence of things will get us out of our crisis. It could feel like solidarity with nonhumans is not enough. We have to do more than that, right? What should we do? Those questions come from the dualistic fixation that puts humans in positions of agents who have to do something to fix the natural world. Looking for something to do to ensure a safe escape from ecological crisis is the karmic situation driving the crisis. However, this does not mean that we should try to escape from our tendency to escape. That is obviously just more of the same problem, more of the same neurotic fixation.

What if efforts to get out of the ecological crisis were preventing us from getting out of ecological crisis? What if trying to get out was precisely what prevented us from getting out?

It is like a Chinese finger trap—a puzzle that you play by putting a finger from one hand in one end of a small, finger-sized tube, and putting a finger from the other hand in the other end. Once your fingers are inside, you cannot pull them out without the trap tightening around your fingers and thus further entrenching you in the trap. To continue struggling against the trap is the dualistic fixation of the self who is opposed to the other, the fixation of humankind struggling against intimacy with nonhumans. The only way out is through—to let go, to release the fixation, to go with the flow. Samsaric energy mutates into compassion. If you let your fingers move further into the trap, the trap relaxes its grip and you can effortlessly free your fingers. Liberation comes from accepting the trap, letting beings be.

A compassionate response to the climate crisis does not mean that you have to worry yourself with obsessive questioning, "What should I do?" It means letting things be, letting yourself be in unbearably intimate relations with nonhumans, letting samsaric energy mutate. It means trusting the process of letting things be, trusting your solidarity with nonhumans, and accepting imperfection. We all make mistakes. Striving to escape that basic impurity only intensifies samsaric energy but does not let it transform. Rather than micromanaging your life or giving constant attention to every single problem, compassionate action lets things be. The courage to be compassionate constitutes a mutation of the karma driving the climate crisis. Chögyam Trungpa puts it simply: "Part of compassion is trust. If something positive is happening, you don't have to check up on it all the time. The more you check up, the more possibilities there are of interrupting the growth. It requires fearlessness to let things be."[15]

Notes

1 Mike Hulme, "(Still) Disagreeing About Climate Change: Which Way Forward?" *Zygon* 50.4 (2015): 897–99.
2 Ulrich Beck, *Risk Society: Towards a New Modernity, trans. Mark Ritter* (SAGE, 1992).
3 Naomi Klein, *This Changes Everything: Capitalism vs. the Climate* (Simon & Schuster, 2014).
4 Naomi Klein, *The Shock Doctrine: The Rise of Disaster Capitalism* (Picador, 2007).
5 Bill McKibben, *Eaarth: Making a Life on a Tough Planet* (Times Books, 2010).
6 Chögyam Trungpa, *The Future Is Open: Good Karma, Bad Karma, and Beyond Karma* (Shambhala, 2018), 3.
7 *Ibid.*, 3–4.
8 Clive Hamilton, *Defiant Earth: The Fate of Humans in the Anthropocene* (Polity Press, 2017), 41.
9 *Ibid.*
10 Timothy Morton, *Dark Ecology: Toward a Logic of Future Coexistence* (Columbia UP, 2016), 24.

11 Timothy Morton, *The Ecological Thought* (Harvard UP, 2010), 50.

12 Timothy Morton, "Thinking Ecology," *Collapse* 6 (2010): 265.

13 Sam Mickey, *Coexistentialism and the Unbearable Intimacy of Ecological Emergency* (Lexington Books, 2016).

14 Friedrich Nietzsche, "Homer's Contest," in *The Nietzsche Reader*, ed. Keith Ansell Pearson and Duncan Large, (Blackwell, 2006), 95.

15 Chögyam Trungpa, *Mindfulness in Action: Making Friends with Yourself through Meditation and Everyday Awareness* (Shambhala, 2015), 56.

Ontological Imagination: An Anzaldúan Manifesto for Social Change

Typically, those of us educated in eurocentric cultures have been taught to define imagination in narrow terms—as an exclusively human faculty associated with fiction, pretense, and unreality—with things that don't exist in three-dimensional, physical space. Imagination's worlds are separate from (and often even an escape from) ordinary reality—the "real world." We're trained to distrust imagination (except in specifically delineated spheres–studying literature, reading fiction, viewing films, and so on); we're instructed to assume that imagination will mislead and deceive us–a suspicion that's existed for centuries, as evidenced by Renee Descartes' description of imagination as "small," "circumscribed," and thus prone to error (*Meditations* 21). In short, western definitions of imagination presume its non-ontological status.

However, these definitions are too limited in scope to describe imagination's powerful, intimate interconnections with multiple realities—including the ordinary reality of our embodied, physical-material-psychic lives. And so, I use the term "ontological imagination" to distinguish it from conventional western versions, to hint at its beyond-human status, and to underscore its intimate engagements *with* reality—especially its ability to intervene in and disrupt injustice. After a brief meditation on ontological imagination, I suggest two foundational practices that can assist us in harnessing its energy to enact progressive social change. As my title might imply, I draw heavily on Gloria Anzaldúa's work to develop this theory because her perspectives on imagination closely correlate with my own. As a queer woman-of-color intellectual-activist, poet, and artist, Anzaldúa approaches imagination with a sense of urgency, forging her theories of dialogue with personal, embodied, psychic experiences of material, systemic oppression. Moreover, reading a short story draft of hers years ago activated my ontological imagination, and I have never been the same.[1]

Imagination is ontological in at least three interrelated ways: First, imagination has an existence of its own; it precedes and exceeds the human. Indeed, perhaps one could say that the human is born into imagination, that imagination contains us, that we're imagination's hands and feet. Anzaldúa alludes to this possibility in her posthumously published book, *Light in the Dark/Luz en lo oscuro: Rewriting Identity, Spirituality, Reality*, when she asserts that:

The mind does not make things up; it just imagines what exists and tells the soul to remember. The soul forgets and must be reminded again and again by signals from nature whose spirits exist in fields, forests, rivers, and other places, and from arrebatamientos (traumatic events). (24)

Here Anzaldúa associates imagination with the ontological, which she contrasts with make-believe, and locates it in the external world; imagination functions as an intellectual faculty that reminds us about previously unavailable aspects of reality ("what exists"). It can do so because it exists in this reality—in our surroundings and in the traumatic events we experience.

Second, ontological imagination inhabits additional levels of reality, what Anzaldúa variously describes (almost in passing) as "nepantla," "the cracks between the worlds," or "the psychic fourth dimension." Henry Corbin, in dialogue with Arabic and Persian philosophers, offers a moresystematic discussion of these additional levels, describing them as "interworlds" or "the eighth climate." Interworlds are as real as the physical world we humans inhabit during most of our daily lives, although we can't sense these worlds with our sensory organs. As Corbin explains, an interworld is "fully objective and real;" it "possesses extension and dimensions, forms and colors, without their being perceptible to the senses, as they are when they are properties of physical bodies." We access this eighth climate through "imaginative perception or the 'psycho-spiritual senses'"—that is, through ontological imagination. To emphasize: we do not create these worlds—worlds that are as real and as "objective" as the conventional world in which we live. We enter these worlds. They precede us.

Third, ontological imagination enables us to reshape reality—a reality that includes (and exceeds) the three-dimensional material world of our daily existence. In part, this intervention occurs through imagination's creative knowledge production. Imagination takes us to other dimensions of reality where we obtain new knowledge, insights, abilities, and partnerships with which to reshape physical-material space. Anzaldúa, borrowing from James Hillman and Corbin, describes these realms as "the imaginal." When we access the imaginal, we encounter nonhuman people and other beings. Importantly, these figures are autonomous—they are not simply representations of our own minds As Anzaldúa explains,

Imagination is the realm of the soul, and the language of the psyche is metaphoric. The imaginal's figures and landscapes are experienced as alive and independent of the dreamer. They speak with their own voices; move about at will. *They possess an intelligence and an inner knowing.* (*Light* 36, my italics)

As this passage suggests, imaginal figures and worlds are not imaginary—they're not make-believe entities that we dream up in the solitary confinement of our limited, individual human minds. Nor do they dwell entirely in our individual unconscious. They have their own lives, ideas, and existence—an existence that goes beyond the personal; they inhabit "the realm of soul"—a pre or beyond-human world soul. As such, they have wisdom and insights that exceed ours. We can work with these insights, using them to enact genuinely new forms of resistance and develop visions of potential futures that do not simply replicate alternative versions of the status quo. To borrow a cliche, ontological imagination enables us to think outside the box. (Indeed, ontological imagination invites us to entirely reconfigure this box.)

I find signs and glimpses of ontological imagination throughout

Anzaldúa's work–in her early poem, "The coming of el mundo sur-do," where she predicts that she and other visionary activists will develop the ability to "walk / through walls;" in her children's book, *La Prieta y la Llorona / Prietita and the Ghost Woman*, where her protagonist encounters an imaginal Llorona who changes her life; in her personal experiences with spirits and encounters with her nagual; in other short stories where shapeshifting, bilocation, and ghostly battles occur; and in her profound relationship with Coyolxauhqui.

So that's the theory, but what's the practice? How might we activate ontological imagination and use it to make progressive social change? At this point, I don't know for sure; I'm trying to live my way into possible answers. In the meantime, I offer two tactics that can serve as groundwork on which to develop our ability to access and use ontological imagination: (1) Posit a metaphysics of radical interconnectedness; and (2) intentionally align ourselves with this interwoven world.

First Tactic:
Posit a Metaphysics of
Radical Interconnectedness

As I define the term, a metaphysics of radical intercon-nectedness is a philosophical system/worldview in which *everything* that exists is interconnected, sacred, and saturated with meaning. All reality emerges from some type of shared ontological ground[2] (or being) that embodies itself throughout—and as—all existence. This fluid cosmic spirit/energy/consciousness (*call it what you will*) is both source and substance; it's the framework and creative force underlying, infusing, and shaping all that exists. I intentionally use a variety of terms to describe this energetic stuff in order to convey my belief that the words we use for labels are far less important than the work it does in the world: its work ensuring our intercon-nectedness–our basic, fundamental relationships–with all existence. And, I describe this interconnectedness as "radical" to underscore the foundational inter-relatedness of everything (visible, invisible, semi-visible; tangible, intangible; physical, nonphysical, etc.) that exists. Or, as Anzaldúa puts it, "Spirit exists in everything; therefore God, the divine, is in everything . . . it's in the tree, the swamp, the sea . . . . Some people call it 'God;' some call it the 'creative force,' whatever. It's in everything" (*Interviews/Entrevistas* 100).

Although western philosophical traditions typically associate "metaphysics" with abstraction, transcendence, and escape from the material, physical world in which we live, I define the term "metaphysics" differently, and use it to underscore spirit's embodied presence—its immanence in (*and as*) materiality. Expressing itself concretely in our daily lives and our surroundings, a metaphysics of radical interconnectedness situates us *here*—in the existing physical-material world and the present moment. In a metaphysics of radical interconnectedness matter/spirit, mind/nature, body/soul, "inner"/"outer" are intertwined layers of a single, complex, interwoven reality—not separate spheres of existence.

Elsewhere, I've discussed how a metaphysics of radical interconnectedness emboldens spiritual activists, fostering self-confidence that can energize, inspire, and embolden our social justice work.[3] Here, I suggest that this radical interconnectivity can bolster imaginal self-trust. In a metaphysics of radical interconnectedness, imagination is not a private, internalized faculty located exclusively (and uniquely) within each human being. Rather, imagination is a shared faculty with a bridging function that—when activated—connects us with other dimensions of reality. We can imaginatively enter into other realms—whether the realm of a snake crossing our path, a squirrel hopping from tree to tree, the trees on which that squirrel pauses, the images in *Light in the Dark*, the metaphor in a poem or a sunset, the spirit we encounter in our dreams, and so on. Relinquishing conscious control, we can rely on imagination to take us into these other worlds and perspectives—to expand our understanding by connecting us with beings/entities/thoughts/ideas that exist outside us. In this imaginal work, our shared commonality with all existence bridges the subject-object divide reified by Cartesian thought while fostering the self-trust necessary to activate ontological imagination. Recognizing this shared commonality enables us to travel into other perspectives.

Because we have something in common with everything that exists, we can obtain useful insights and wisdom from our surroundings—from the human and nonhuman people we encounter–or what intellectual-activist adrienne marie brown calls "the sacred systems of life all around us" (kindle loc. 30). We activate these systems by acknowledging their existence *as* wisdom systems and by paying increased attention to them. Through this attention, we obtain insights, instructions, and lessons that we can implement in various ways. As Anzaldúa instructs us: "Read the present moment; whatever you need to learn about life is written there" (*Light* 179). Reading the present moment is part of the second tactic: intentional alignment.

Second Tactic: Intentional Alignment

I define intentional alignment as the act of establishing a self-reflective, dialogic relationship with spirit—the same spirit (though called by many names) that runs through all existence and ensures our radical interconnectedness. Alignment begins by positing our radical interconnectedness with all existence and recognizing that this interconnectedness functions epistemologically and ethically, guiding us each day. We align ourselves with the external world by positing its spirit-infused quality and reading our interactions for messages that we co-create with the people (plant people, snake people, rock people, and so on) that we encounter.

When we're in alignment, we consciously recognize, activate, and trust our intimate interconnection with spirit as we live our lives and move through the world. Our metaphysics of radical interconnectedness (the first tactic) ensures our innate divinity and our shared source; we align ourselves with this innate divinity by acknowledging and opening ourselves to its presence. We heed our surroundings; we look for synchronicities, commonalities, patterns, and harmonies.

When we intentionally align ourselves with the cosmos, we read our surroundings and the events in our lives for messages from Spirit, and we use imagination to interpret Spirit's "words." We know that the things that come to us (random thoughts, a passage in a book, events in our lives), that linger in the back of our minds, contain information and insights we can access by paying attention, listening, and trusting the insights we receive/co-create. Put differently: We enter into dialogue and trust our interpretations. Anzaldúa illustrates one of the many forms these dialogic encounters can take in the final chapter of *Light in the Dark*, where she begins by recounting her daily walks across Lighthouse Field, a small national park located near her home in Santa Cruz, CA. Here's how the chapter opens:

> As you walk across Lighthouse Field a glistening black ribbon undulates in the grass, crossing your path from right to left. You swallow air, your primal senses flare open. From the middle of your forehead, a reptilian eye blinks, surveys the terrain. This visual intuitive sense, like the intellect of heart and gut, reveals a discourse of signs, images, feelings, words that, once decoded, carry the power to startle you out of tunnel vision and habitual patterns of thought. The snake is a symbol of awakening consciousness—the potential of knowing within, an awareness and intelligence not grasped by logical thought. Often nature provokes un "aja," or "conocimiento," one that guides your feet along the path, gives you el ánimo to dedicate yourself to transforming perceptions of reality, and thus the conditions of life. (117)

Anzaldúa establishes an intimate interrelationship between herself and her surroundings. Importantly, this relationship is reciprocal and dialogic—a nonverbal conversation co-initiated by Anzaldúa and her surroundings: As a "glistening black" snake crosses her path, the sinuous movement invites her to shift into an "intellect of heart and gut." As she inhales, she "swallow[s] air" and the outer world enters her, thus facilitating an embodied epistemological shift: her "primal senses flare open" and alter her perception. Anzaldúa underscores the unconventional (to Cartesian thinkers) nature of this holistic perceptual shift by linking it with the sixth chakra (also called the third eye and located in the middle of the forehead) and describing it as "a reptilian eye," a "visual intuitive sense," an "awakening consciousness," and internal knowledge.

As her consciousness awakens, Anzaldúa moves from modernity's restrictive thinking (here described as "tunnel vision," "habitual patterns of thought," and "logical thought") into a more expansive, relational mode of thinking which give her access to a world that communicates in "a discourse of signs, images, feelings, words" that she can now read. Everything she encounters has a spirit-infused sacred quality: "You experience nature as ensouled, as sacred" (117). This experience transforms Anzaldúa's work as an author and social-justice activist, inspiring her to approach it as an offering to spirit: "Éste saber, this knowledge, urges you to cast una ofrenda of images and words across the page como granos de maize, like kernels of corn." Anzaldúa further underscores this participatory relationship by initiating an exchange between herself and spirit: "You stop in the middle of the field and, under your breath, ask the spirits—animals, plants, y tus muertos—to help you string together a bridge of words. What follows is your attempt to give back to nature, los espíritus, and others a gift wrested from the events in your life, a bridge home to the self" (117). Anzaldúa uses ritual (she casts an offering) and prayer to further deepen the reciprocal relationship between herself and a spirit-infused world.

As we see throughout *Light in the Dark*, Anzaldúa's point is not simply to establish a more profound relationship between herself and the outer/inner worlds but rather to use this relationship ontologically, in order to enter "imaginal realities" (34) and use what she learns to transform *this* world. These imaginal realities are not simply the products of her personal imagination but rather represent transpersonal (and transhuman) psychic realms in which transformation can occur. More specifically, she enters the imaginal, gains new insights (and partnerships), and then uses what she's learned to transform material reality through her cutting-edge, provocative texts.[4]

Alignment can unfold in additional ways as well–ranging from self-reflective perceptual engagement with our surroundings to a wide variety of spiritual practices and technologies (prayer, ritual, affirmation, ceremony) as well as ancient esoteric wisdom traditions (astrology, numerology, the I Ching, and Tarot), or what Toni Cade Bambara describes as "everybody's ancient wisdom." We can use these various spiritual technologies to intentionally put ourselves into harmony with these cosmic patterns; engage in new dialogues; gain new insights, inspiration, and energy; and use what we've learned to make change in the ordinary daily world.

Ontological imagination invites us to exceed ourselves, to move beyond conventional beliefs about reality. When we use imagination ontologically, we dream boldly and question that which seems to be "realistic"–especially when reality has been defined by the Cartesian framework's status-quo. Encompassing contradiction, complexity, paradox, and the so-called supernatural, ontological imagination enables us to challenge this restrictive status quo and dream new, more equitable realities into existence.

Notes & Works Cited

1   I summarize this transformative experience in my article, "Speculative Realism, Visionary Pragmatism."
2   I use the word "ground," rather than "essence," to describe this ontological foundation because "ground" is more tangible, more closely linked with the physical-material world/earth.
3   See my book, *Transformation Now! Towards a Post-Oppositional Politics of Change.*
4   For information on Anzaldúa's life and social justice work, see the first two chapters of my book, *The Anzaldúan Theory Handbook.*

Anzaldúa, Gloria. "The coming of el mundo surdo." 1977. *The Gloria Anzaldúa Reader*, ed. A. Keating, Duke UP, 2009, 36–37.
——. *Interviews/Entrevistas*, edited by A. Keating, Routledge, 2000.
——. *Light in the Dark/Luz en lo oscuro: Rewriting Identity, Spirituality, Reality*, edited by A. Keating, Duke UP, 2015.
——. *Prietita and the Ghost Woman/ Prietita y La Llorona*, Children's Book Press, 1995.
brown, adrienne marie. *Emergent Strategy: Shaping Change, Changing Worlds.* AK Press, 2017.
Corbin, Henri. "Mundus Imaginalis, or the Imaginary and the Imaginal." 1964. *Swedenborg and Esoteric Islam.* Trans. Leonard Fox. Swedenborg Foundation, 1995.
Descartes, René. "Meditations On First Philosophy," 1641 Internet Encyclopedia of Philosophy, 1996. This file is of the 1911 edition of *The Philosophical Works of Descartes* (Cambridge UP). Trans. E. S. Haldan.
Keating, AnaLouise. *The Anzaldúan Theory Handbook*, Duke UP, 2022.
——. "Speculative Realism, Visionary Pragmatism, and Poet-Shamanic Aesthetics in Gloria Anzaldúa–and Beyond." *Women's Studies Quarterly* 40.3/4 (2012): 51–69.
——. *Transformation Now! Toward a Post-Oppositional Politics of Change*, University of Illinois Press, 2013.

Manifesto of a Gaian Cosmology

AUTHOR'S NOTE: The original version of this essay was published on my blog on March 23, 2020, twelve days after the World Health Organization declared the COVID-19 outbreak a global pandemic. I've edited and expanded the version below in an effort to amplify its core message to better meet the current somewhat mutated conditions of late 2023.

A SPECTER IS HAUNTING our nascent planetary civilization—the specter of Gaia. All the powers of the global capitalist market have entered into a holy alliance to exorcise this specter. Even sworn enemies agree Gaia must be subdued, made to conform to the quartly projections of the global economy.

While they may still call Her by other names, like Climate Change or The Environmental Crisis or COVID-19, the nation-states and transnationals all by now acknowledge and fear Gaia's power. But they continue to obscure the consequences of a profit-maximizing, extractive algorithm that is rapidly driving our species and many besides off an extinction cliff. Humanity can no longer ignore but must face Gaia head and heart on. It is past time for Gaians—those who refuse the role of corporate employee-costumer and instead commit to cultivating a more ecological mode of planetary coexistence—to make themselves publicly known by telling a truer story of this planet and our purpose here.

The history of all hitherto existing human society emerges from the history of Earth and cosmic evolution.

Star and atom, galaxy and planet, animal and single cell, in a word, symbiotic organisms, danced in mutual interplay with one another for billions of years, giving rise to our species and its fragile civilization, now increasingly divided into those who want to inhabit this planet and those who insist on escape from all Her limits.

The name "Gaia" is borrowed from the scientific hypothesis of James Lovelock, who himself borrowed it from author William Golding, who in turn borrowed it from Hesiod's telling of ancient Greek cosmogony. Do not imagine an anthropomorphized goddess, "Mother Nature," when you hear this term. Imagine instead a complex community of coevolving lifeforms participating in the maintenance of a self-organizing network of geochemical feedback loops. The habitability of this planet—for humans as for all other creatures—depends upon the relative stability of this nexus of relations. For several hundred years, this living Earth has been treated as a mere background to human activity, a storehouse of raw materials to be violently exploited, a passive stage upon which our technological progress could unfold indefinitely, a gigantic dumping ground for our toxic waste. But Gaia could not be dispelled by the industrial might or monetary magic of global capitalism. Gaia has only been further provoked by it.

Despite the wishful thinking of capitalist economists, the market is not a "perpetual motion machine"[1] insulated from the biophysical inevitabilities of entropy and extinction. Since the end of the last ice age 12,000 years ago, the human economy has always existed at the grace of Earth's ecology. Whether agricultural, industrial, or informational, our species has undertaken each new mode of production with tremendous Promethean creativity. And each time we have ignored or downplayed the geophysiological consequences of our innovations.

"Gaia's intrusion,"[2] as the philosopher Isabelle Stengers has referred to it, has always been inevitable, but until very recently, it was for the most part only decipherable scientifically through complex data sets and computer simulations of global temperature rise, biodiversity loss, and many other relatively abstract metrics detailing the fraying of Her feedback loops. Timelines stretching to the end of this century warned of the dire consequences of failing to take bold action to curb greenhouse gas emissions and reverse other ecologically unsustainable practices. Insurance companies were beginning to feel uneasy about the increasing severity of droughts, wildfires, and hurricanes, but surely Gaia could wait for the market to adapt.

Today the situation is quickly mutating from future possibility into present emergency. After a decades-long trial period, planetary transformation is now no longer optional: "we do not have any choice, because [Gaia] will not wait."[3]

What remained a specter only a few years ago—a barely perceptible threat safely hidden behind the noise and smog of business as usual—has now brought the entirety of modern human civilization to an evolutionary impasse. Recent economic downturns have meant that most of the world's human population remains unable to consume or produce at the ever-increasing rates required of a capitalist system.

Marxist philosopher Fredric Jameson once said that "it is easier to imagine the end of the world than to imagine the end of capitalism."[4] Jameson's statement was borrowed from H. Bruce Franklin, whose original utterance was composed as a question: "What could [our species] create if [we] were able to envision the end of capitalism as not the end, but the beginning, of a human world?"[5] With the old world now on the brink as humanity is brought to its knees by Gaia—the for-too-long-taken-for-granted ground beneath our feet—our species has a fateful decision to make. Will we continue to pray to the God of the Market by imposing another round of what Naomi Klein has called "disaster capitalism," or might we invoke an older god?

To Marxist ears, the invocation of a god, especially one with the mythic residue of "Gaia," resounds of ideology. Why leave our capitalist chains behind only to succumb to a new, or ancient, opiate of the masses? Worse, my narrative account of our current situation as the disruption of the human political economy due to the intrusion of a seemingly outside natural power appears to be a textbook case of the process Roland Barthes warned about more than half a century ago, whereby "the bourgeoisie transforms the reality of the world into an image of the world, History into Nature";[6] this, according to Barthes, is "the very principle of myth: it transforms history into nature."[7]

But Gaia has not come in any form recognized by the terms of the modern constitution, signed by Marxists and capitalists alike, which placed a metaphysical chasm between human society and physical nature: the historical realization of freedom on one side, mere matter to be mastered by it on the other. "If man is shaped by the environment," Marx wrote, "his environment must be made human."[8] Even Marx's dialectical materialism remains largely insensitive to Gaia's non-modern mode of composition. Gaia is not "The Environment," not "Nature" as modern people have conceived of it. Gaia does not passively suffer our historical projects. Nor has Gaia come in the ancient form imagined by our ancestors. Gaia is not natural and not mythical. Gaia is a geohistorical hybrid, to use Bruno Latour's favored definition.[9] Latour asks us to face Gaia not as a transcendent mythical or immanent natural unifier, but as a call to return to concrete, earthbound existence as members of a Whiteheadian democracy of fellow creatures. Gaia is just as much an agent of history as human beings.

Finding ways to get along with the bizarre biological neighbors modernity has for several centuries prided itself on ignoring will not be easy, as the recent and still unfolding COVID-19 pandemic exemplifies. Human survival in this new/old Gaian reality will require reimagining our political,[10] religious,[11] scientific,[12] and artistic[13] forms. Our concept of society will need to be expanded to include non-humans. Time itself will need restorying: History has always been ending; myth endlessly beginning; and creation forever ongoing. We are not rational actors driven instinctively to calculate profit and loss in advance of our exchanges. We are not lords of the land and owners of private property. We are coevolving creatures like all others, bound by a single atmosphere, kin with the bacteria that fertilize the soil, with the wheat and fruiting trees, with the flower pollinating bees, with all the other fungi, plants, and animals populating this planet. Becoming Gaian is not so much a matter of reinventing ourselves as "merely" biological organisms as of shedding our god-like Promethean ambitions, of learning to settle down here on the earth beneath the sky instead of setting sail once more, this time beyond all finite horizons, as if Mars, too, could be colonized and commodified. Humans do have a unique ecological role, but we cannot recover it so long as an economic logic of extraction continues to supersede the ecological fact of our interdependence with all life. Despite the theoretical dualisms of the modern world view, the capitalist economy cannot escape its biophysical conditions to achieve perpetual motion. Contrary to Jeff Bezos and Elon Musk, our species is not destined for space capitalism. All that is solid has not melted into air. Even the "cloud" that hosts our digital economy depends upon massive super-cooled server farms and undersea cables to power and distributed its invisible information network.

Marx and Engels could not have foreseen the specific condition—a new human-caused geological epoch and climatic condition—that would finally initiate the dialectical self-overcoming of capitalism. But they did predict that capitalism, by expanding the market over the entire surface of the globe and establishing connections everywhere, would at last compel each of us to face with sober senses our real conditions of life, and our true relations to others of our kind. Our conditions of life, and our shared vulnerability, have never been more apparent than during the recent planetary quarantine due to the COVID-19 pandemic. Millions of people found themselves in need of medical care, and billions more needed an economic lifeline. All humanity, despite our social distancing and our cultural diversity, was united against a common enemy, at least for a moment. But who is this enemy? COVID-19? If we are no longer modern, we cannot so easily disentangle ourselves from this viral agent, as though "Nature" had raised a microscopic army against us. After all, maybe *we* are the virus. Maybe COVID-19 is a Gaian antibody... *Nonsense*: we, too, are Gaians. We, too, have a place on this planet, if only we would learn to inhabit it more humbly.

What would it mean to be civilized in a humbler non-modern, or ecological way? For Whitehead, civilization implies beings capable of consciously striving for the historical realization of transformative ideas, including freedom and love. Whitehead is not an idealist, however. He is an organic realist. Ideas can only exert power when the material and historical conditions are ripe, when a particular habitat is capable of supporting their ingression.

Many moderns, Marx included, have too anthropocentric an idea of ideas. Ideas were already active in evolutionary processes long before conscious human beings emerged on the scene. Ideas are not just conjured up in human heads. Whitehead's philosophy of organism is an invitation to consider the possibility that the idea of the Good participates in generating the light and warmth of the Sun no less than the nuclear reactions and electromagnetic radiation known to physicists; that the idea of Beauty is at work in the evolution of peacocks, butterflies, and roses and not just in Beethoven's 9th or the Mona Lisa. Ideas don't just shape history, they shape geostory and cosmogenesis as a whole.

Whitehead: "The basis of democracy is the common fact of value-experience, as constituting the essential nature of each pulsation of actuality. Everything has some value for itself, for others, and for the whole."[14] Every bacterium enriching the soil, every bumble bee making honey in the hive, every human laboring at home or in a factory, every star spiraling in the galaxy has value for itself, for others, and for the whole. Nonhumans not only *have* value, but they are also agents of value creation.

What is value? Debates continue to rage among economists about the differences between use and exchange value, or between objective and subjective value, but under capitalist social relations, Marx locates value in a social relation determined by the amount of labor time required to produce a commodity. The implication is that only humans create value by working on raw material or nature.

Is all value really produced by human labor alone? Is there nothing extra-human that supplies value? In Whitehead's cosmos—and the Gaian reality moderns are confronting, or being confronted by—there is no more mere matter or dead nature, no inert or raw material to be appropriated by someone called Man. "We have no right," Whitehead admonishes us, "to deface the value-experience which is the very essence of the universe."[15] Value is typically linked to agency. Moderns, whether Locke, Marx, or Hayek, have limited agency and thus value creation to human beings (or worse, as within capitalist social relations, value creation is even further delimited to those lucky or forceful enough to be owners of capital).

Despite his recognition of metabolic rift, Marx was fully modern in his commitment to what Latour calls the double task of emancipation and domination.[16] The emancipatory task was political: to end exploitation of humans by humans. The task of domination was techno-scientific: to become masters of nature.

Gaia's intrusion is turning the irreality of the modern lifestyle upside down and inside out. We are beginning to see and feel ourselves surrounded by Gaia, swallowed, trapped. We cannot escape to a beyond but are earthbound, Musk and Bezos' extra-terrestrial utopianism notwithstanding.

We must re-think human freedom and our planetary condition as though Gaia mattered. Humans are not as free and teleological as moderns have imagined; nor is nature as dumb and aimless. Marx said that the worst human architect is distinguished from the best honeybee by the fact that the former designs his building ideally before constructing it materially. Man has a plan. Bees, apparently, are simply automatons obeying blind instinct. But is this really how human or insect creativity works? Organic architect Christopher Alexander[17] studied how medieval cathedrals were generated over generations in a purposeful but not centrally planned way. This is akin to the way insects build their nests, following a simple organizational patterning language out of which emerges enduring forms of beauty. Buildings that are designed and built in the way Marx imagined tend to be dead structures with a deadening influence upon their inhabitants. Consciousness of the power of ideas does not mean mastery over ideas. Ideas possess us, purpose us; we participate in their power, coworkers and not free inventors.

Where to go from here? In place of deterministic teleology, we need processes of relational creativity. In place of individual competition and class hierarchy, a creaturely democracy and social solidarity with and beyond human beings. In place of a Big Plan from on high, playful kin-making with the community of nonhuman beings we breathe, eat, love, and otherwise share this planet with. Instead of providential history, we must settle for what anthropologist James Clifford calls "big enough" stories that remain ontologically unfinished, situated in contact zones, sites of struggle and dialogue.

We need new practices of aestheticization, new stories, new rituals (or perhaps we need to respectfully recover old practices, stories, and rituals) to help sensitize us to the values of nonhumans. Our survival depends on it.

Becoming sensitive to the values of nonhumans doesn't mean rejecting a hierarchy of values that in many cases gives humans pride of place. As Whitehead says, "life is robbery." But, he continues, "the robber needs justification."[18] What is the human, anyway? Are we one species among many? In an obvious sense, of course we are; and we ignore our dependence upon and embeddedness within wider ecological networks to our own peril. In another sense, we are not just another species. We have become, for better or worse, a planetary presence, a geological force. How are we to justify our dominant presence on Earth? What does ecological justice look like when the idea of justice is expanded beyond just human society? These are questions any civilization hoping to survive the next century is going to need to address.

Human history is no less a spiritual than a geophysical event. Whether we date the history of this event to the emergence of symbolic consciousness 200,000 years ago, the Neolithic revolution 12,000 years ago, the capitalist revolution 500 years ago, the industrial revolution 250 years ago, the nuclear age 75 years ago, or the information age only several decades ago, it is clear that the Earth community has by now at least entered a new phase of geohistorical development. Whether we call it the Anthropocene, the Capitalocene, the Plantationocene, the Chthulucene, the Entropocene, or the Ecozoic, diagnosing the metaphysical root of the present ecological catastrophe is a necessary (though not sufficient) part of imagining and materializing a post-capitalist world.

Marx, of course, was not unaware of our profound connection to the Earth: "Nature is man's *inorganic* body, that is to say, nature in so far as it is not the human body. Man *lives* from nature…and he must maintain a continuing dialogue with it if he is not to die. To say that man's physical and mental life is linked to nature simply means that nature is linked to itself, for man is a part of nature."[19] In *Capital*, he writes of labor as a process "by which man, through his own actions, mediates, regulates, and controls the metabolism between himself and nature. He confronts the materials of nature as a force of nature." I do not mean to downplay the extent to which Marx's dialectical understanding of the Human-Earth relation goes a long way toward describing our new Gaian reality. But he still could not shake the all too modern tendency to treat Earth as dead and awaiting the value-creating power of human consciousness. So with Whitehead, I have argued that value is not just a human social construct or free creation of human labor or desire (modern thinkers as diverse as Locke, Marx, and Hayek agree on this) but a cosmological power from which our human values, and our human power, derives.

Notes

1   Neil Irwin, "One Simple Idea That Explains Why the Economy Is in Great Danger," *The New York Times*, March 17th, 2020. https://www.nytimes.com/2020/03/17/upshot/coronavirus-economy-crisis-demand-shock.html
2   Isabelle Stengers, *In Catastrophic Times*, 50. https://meson.press/wp-content/uploads/2015/11/978-1-78542-010-8_In-Catastrophic-Times_Stengers.pdf
3   *Ibid.*
4   Fredric Jameson, "Future City," *New Left Review* 21 (May/June 2003): 76. Credit is due to Matthew Beaumont for pointing out Jameson's sources: see "Imagining the End Times: Ideology, the Contemporary Disaster Movie, Contagion" in *Zizek and Media Studies: A Reader* (2014).
5   Franklin, "What are we to make of J.G. Ballard's Apocalypse?"; https://www.jgballard.ca/criticism/ballard_apocalypse_1979.html.
6   Roland Barthes, "Myth Today," in *Mythologies*, trans. Annette Lavers, (Vintage, 1993), 141.

7 *Ibid.*, 129.

8 The Holy Family, Chapter 6, Part 3 (D): Critical Battle Against French Materialism https://www.marxists.org/subject/dialectics/marx-engels/holy-family.htm#:~:text=If%20man%20is%20shaped%20by,by%20the%20power%20of%20society

9 See especially Latour, *Facing Gaia* (2017) and *We Have Never Been Modern* (1993)

10 https://footnotes2plato.com/2018/10/26/schellings-philosophy-of-freedom/

11 https://matthewsegall.files.wordpress.com/2013/06/religion-in-human-and-cosmic-evolution-whiteheads-alternative-vision-publication-copy.pdf

12 See M.D. Segall, *Physics of the World-Soul: Whitehead's Adventure in Cosmology* (SacraSage, 2021).

13 See Segall, MD, "The Function of Reason and the Recovery of an Earthly Architecture" in *720* by Function Lab, Iss. 12 (2016): https://matthewsegall.files.wordpress.com/2023/05/e2808efunctionlab.netwp-contentuploads201606720_the-function-of-reason-and-the-recovery-of-an-earthly-architecture-1.pdf

14 Whitehead, *Modes of Thought* (The Free Press, 1938), 111.

15 *Ibid.*

16 Bruno Latour, *We Have Never Been Modern* (1991), 10.

17 https://thesideview.co/journal/restoring-architectures-cosmic-context/

18 Whitehead, *Process and Reality* (The Free Press, 1978), 105.

19 Karl Marx, "Estranged Labor" (1844).

BARBARA KARLSEN

Becoming Metamorphic
Moving Towards a New Conception of Life

The Word may come to us from within; it may come to us from without. But in either case, it is only an agency for setting the hidden knowledge to work. The word within may be the utterance of the inmost soul in us which is always open to the Divine or it may be the word of the secret and universal Teacher who is seated in the hearts of all. — Sri Aurobindo[1]

WHEN I FIRST MET EMILIE CONRAD in the early '90s the idea that our body was an unfolding aspect of the biosphere was so counterculture. A somatic visionary ahead of her time she coined the term *"species inclusion"* to refer to the way our evolutionary biological heritage encompassed the interweaving of all life forms that came before.[2] It was an evolutionary heritage spanning bacteria, fungi, plant, and animal, with no visible transition in between. Now three decades later, her somatic knowing is a scientific reality thanks to the Human Genome project. Not only are we a human species composed of human cells, genes, tissues, and organs, but living in us and on us, are over 500 species of organisms, encoding 100 times more unique genes than our own genome. What's more, there is an ancient fluid matrix linking the DNA of every cell inside the body, including the microbiome. After thousands of years thinking we were a separate human species, it is clear we are an immense outpouring of the Cosmos. It is no longer a science fiction fantasy; it is molecular, cellular, and visceral, scientific reality.

This major shift in our scientific understanding has vast implications for expanding the notion of what we call a human body, towards what we call a planetary, or even a cosmic body. Add to this *our unlimited capacity for plasticity* and you get ontology for re-making ourselves at the species level. It may seem odd that we

need to re-make ourselves, but the fact is we humans have already become something else. After centuries of mechanistic science, hyper-
rationalism, and now technology on a grand scale, we no longer
identify with the web of life that shaped us. We are alienated from
the natural world, the natural rhythms of our body, and the impulse
to move our body in a variety of natural ways. This radical change,
coupled with overuse of antibiotics and the mass spraying of syn-
thetic pesticides, has brought untold ecological carnage—the greatest threat of which is to our biological selves. As of this writing, we
are just through two years of the worst global pandemic our planet
has experienced in more than 100 years. A pandemic that failed
to be contained as we continue to experience breakthrough infec-
tions despite the rollout of ongoing vaccinations. What's more, we
are experiencing the most profound explosion of cancer and chronic
illness in human history. It is clear: something is terribly wrong,
and the problem is not our genes. Our human genes have remained
constant over the last 40,000 years. What has changed drastically
is our lifestyle. We are cut off from our evolutionary past. In other
words we are no longer in alignment with the biological design of
our species.

What follows from this is the need for a radical shift—no less
than a *metamorphosis*—as we resynthesize the dualistically organized body into one that is more fluid, malleable, and entangled with
the web of life, inside and out. Stated simply, without a metamorphosis we remain trapped in a dualistically organized body which
creates false barriers to the complexity of life. This dualistic body is
further reinforced with a conceptual framework that has binaries,
divisions, and even taxonomies, all of which are incongruent with
the new science. In fact, the new science tells us that our human cells
are irreducibly entangled with a mix of fungal, bacterial, and viral relations that preceded our human genome by billions of years. It also
tells us they are bathed within an ancient fluid matrix which has the
memory of all the genomic codes and morphologies that have come
before. These new discoveries in biology were simply unknown a
mere two decades ago. So, when we marry all of these new scientific

elements together, there is no telling what we can become. Longevity is no longer the goal. The emphasis shifts towards the human we are becoming in a new planetary future.

The Body as a Metamorphic Zone

It was through many years of intensive work with Emile Conrad and the practice of Continuum movement that I came to know the body as a womb, or container, through which the mover could be re-born. Unlike most movement practices which consist of following linear instructions or exercising specific body parts, Continuum is a movement practice in learning how to *dissolve* and continually *become*. This alchemical formula of dissolving (*sol*) and becoming (*gel*), which is a central theme in Emilie's work, was never in the interest of becoming something new. Rather, it was always in the interest of dismantling the familiar body we knew and broadening the depth of our embodied experience. For Emile, this embodied experience was inseparable from the Earth, water, trees, plants, and microbes from which it is woven. In fact, she coined the term "*species inclusion*" to describe the way in which our biological heritage encompassed the interweaving of all life forms that came before. It didn't matter if we were looking at a fully developed human, or the infinitesimal goings-on of cells, genes, or microbes; all life was entangled within an interconnected web of becoming.

Situating her work within the context of systems theory, Emile taught that what we call a body is movement. It is a series of unfolding forms that can both make us and un-make us. For example: take the familiar body we know, divide it into parts, and then force it to sit in a chair all day. In all likelihood, you will crush the very plasticity your body has been built for. Take the same body and drape it over the side of a chair, and you get a seeping wetland of complex life. The point is, there is nothing *static* about our anatomy. Our bodies will flow, seep, and change to fit our ecological niche. When we repeat the same movements over and over again, we forfeit our capacity to become something new. In *Life on Land* (2007), Emile asserts:

For years I've been teaching that what we call a body is basically movement that has coalesced in order to live in this particular electromagnetic field. I see our bodies as interpenetrating wave motions that have stabilized "in time" in order to survive successfully on this planet. I see that these wave patterns are of various intervals—some short, others longer. We are matter doing time.[3]

Faced with a Western culture of bodily estrangement and chair sitting, Emile built an entire system for de-constructing the dualistic body and revealing a much deeper body of fluid dimensionality and flow. In this deeper body, the separation between mind and body fell away, and one felt related to all bodies in the biosphere. The feeling of an arm could suddenly interchange with the sense of a wing, or the feeling of a hand could suddenly feel like a fin. "We are moving water, brought to land," Emile writes. "Our bodies contain the memories of all life that has ever been. A claw, a fin, a hand are all blueprints in this biomorphic plane." What Emile taught, and science is now confirming is that our body is the continuation of a universal unfolding; an unbroken biological thread that can be traced to a single ancestor (LUCA), which emerged from the primordial sea 3.5 to 3.8 billion years ago. In other words, our human cells exist because of an incredibly resilient *germline* that has been replicating since the ancient beginnings of life on Earth. Going one step further, Emile taught that the water inside our cells held the memory of all ancestral life that came before. Our bodies are a living continuity across time and space; a sort of space-time-gravity matrix connecting all species, timelines and codes. Emile writes:

We are an accrual of many life forms that have been shaped by our oceanic origins, still pulsating as the intrinsic world of our organs, our connective tissue, our nerve fiber. Our forms have been designed and redesigned, unendingly adaptive, and innovative.[4]

Asking questions such as *"what is a body?"* Emile's classes could be described as a cross between movement exploration and biohacking. Class content could include anything from a descent into human origins to an exploration of microtubules. Movements were often a combination of fluid undulations interspersed with upside down inversions, such as hanging off the seat of a chair. With this practice, cellular fluids could flow forwards and backwards, regenerating whole new cosmologies of life. The future does not arrive ahead of us, Emile taught. It arrives within us, through the ancient primordial sea in which we live and have our origins. When we slow down and linger there, taxonomic divisions dissolve, and complex assemblages show up everywhere. We have access to a more fluid form of intelligence that spans all genus, phylum, and kingdoms.

Unlike traditional anatomy, Emile's anatomy included the water that flowed inside and around our cells. Emile described this water as a *moving anatomy*, a liquid crystalline gel that could flow, seep, and spatially re-arrange itself according to movement. For example, habitual movement would cause this liquid crystalline water to thicken and solidify, whereas dynamic movement would cause the liquid crystalline water to disperse and flow. Stated simply, the water inside our cells has the capacity to undergo a phase transition—from *gel* to *sol*—as it drives all processes within the cell. Unfortunately, prolonged sitting causes this transition to jam, stagnating water inside and outside the cell. In the course of her work, Emile discovered that movement could drive this phase transition, and so Continuum movement was born. In *Life on Land* Emile writes:

When we heighten fluid activities intrinsically—circulation, intercellular fluid, cerebrospinal fluid, interstitial fluid—we are heightening resonance with the fluid body in toto. In this domain of heightened fluid resonance, the organism changes its structure, becoming more generalized, larger in scope. In this fluid heightening, the organism returns once again to its pre-structural cosmic existence, its dreamtime. In this manner, it is echoing the transitional character of the cell, which also changes its form depending on the consistency of its internal fluid structure (gel-sol).[5]

Although Emile's understanding of the water inside our cells may have been well ahead of her time, it was Gerald Pollack who identified the water inside our cells as the 4th *phase of water*. Pollak discovered that the water inside our cells had an extra hydrogen atom (H302), which made it behave very differently than regular water (H20). On the one hand, this water delivered important information and nutrients to the cell, yet it could also quickly rearrange its atoms to squeeze toxins from the cell. Interestingly enough, this biological water also had the capacity to read DNA, fold proteins and capture biophotons from the sun. This was the consciousness of water that intrigued Emilie Conrad. "We may never really know the profundity of water," Emile wrote, "It may well be beyond our capacity to understand the enormity of this compelling substance."[6]

In a Western culture obsessed with personal wounding and pathology, Emile taught that the water in our cells held a universal story. It was the great connector of all species, genes, timelines and codes. In the somatic framework that is Continuum, there is no emphasis on one's personal narrative or story. Instead, the mover's own body intelligence is called forth. Teaching her students to slow down and rest deeply in the field of fluid oneness that bathes every cell, Emile provided a morphic zone for dissolution and plasticity. Quoting Eliade, she adds:

Immersion in water symbolizes a return to the preformal, a total regeneration, a new birth, for immersion in water means a dissolution of forms, a reintegration into the formlessness of pre-existence; and emerging from the water is a repetition of the act of creation in which form was first expressed.[7]

While fluidity is the heart of Continuum movement, the other core principle is the mutability of form (plasticity). These two principles were highly interfused for Emile, and she used them interchangeably to describe the dynamics of emerging form. To illustrate this point, she would often use the example of the developing embryo. Even without having precise instructions from its genes, the embryo is nonetheless able to bring forth its entire body through a fluid process of bending, folding, twisting and invaginating. Sheets of cells roll inward and outward, creating the heart and the gut. Small swellings emerging here and there, forming arteries, organs, and even bones. Following this logic, it becomes clear why plasticity plays a critical role in the unfoldment of biological form. This is because what is what is forming may have to fold, bulge, dissolve boundaries, or intersect across multiple layers at once as it brings forth something new. Without plastcity there would be no new relationship between the parts, boundaries would remain the same, and forms would not change. In short, plasticity continues to do for the body what it does for the embryo. It reassembles everything that is already there. Unlike genes which convey only genetic instructions, plasticity is the basis of emerging form.

Knowing that the dominant notions of embodiment in the West were anchored in dissociation and habitual movement, Emile established three anatomies (fluid, primordial, cosmic) to counteract cultural conditioning. Concerned with the effects of environmental pollution and technology upon the body, she developed Continuum movement to experiment with tissue structure and plasticity. Interested less in chiseled form and more in movement characterized by wave form, Emile was fascinated with the movement of the octopus. She felt its undulating, tentacular movements demonstrated the perfect process for expunging toxins, and so she continually reminded her students to move like water. After all, we are 70% water by volume and 93% water by molecular structure. Putting emphasis on our unused morphological potential, Emile felt that the human species was capable of much more complex orders of existence than we were living.

In *Life on Land*, Emile asserts

Wave motion is a fundamental healer in which all aspects of our existence can move with greater communication. Increasing wave motion permits greater possibility for biological life to communicate with itself. Fluid movement enhances health and wellbeing and has far-reaching benefits beyond our capacity to name.[8]

For Emile, the water inside and around our cells was as much a cosmology as it was a consciousness. As an interrelated whole, the water inside our cells tied together eleven organ systems and five kingdoms of life (Eubacteria, Fungi, Archaebacteria, Protista,

Animalia, and Plantæ). It was a crystalline web of everything: from the chromosomal to the cosmos. Acting like a stored library of genetic and pre-genetic information, the water inside our cells was a key mechanism by which information progressively complexified and materialized. From this place, the body becomes a quantum whole, capable of expressing new degrees of agency hitherto unseen. It seems what Emile taught is now timely and true. We are in new terrain. And as one set of codes for living are coming undone, others are re-assembling. As we slip out of the linear laws of reductionist science and into a whole new quantum order, what will be required is a metamorphic zone for the emergence of something new—a new body, a new form, or a new way of being. And indeed, there are many close links between Continuum movement and what we see in biological metamorphosis.

Much like metamorphosis, Continuum movement provides an exploratory zone for the creation of new shapes and configurations. In other words, it provides a metamorphic zone for the dualistic body to be reshaped and reconceived. In addition, it offers the possibility of experientially understanding new concepts like plasticity, sympoeisis, and morphogenesis. With this kind of conscious, embodied participation available to us, there is room for personal agency and self-directed transformation. The focus shifts from a practice of "biohacking" the human we are *now*, to creating the kind of human that already belongs to a planetary future.

Notes

1 Sri Aurobindo, *The Synthesis of Yoga* (Sri Aurobindo Ashram Press, 1999), 48–49.
2 Emilie Conrad, *Life on Land* (North Atlantic, 2007), 3.
3 *Ibid.*, 249.
4 *Ibid.*, 290.
5 *Ibid.*, 4.
6 *Ibid.*, xxiii.
7 *Ibid.*, 247.
8 *Ibid.*, 143.

SEAN KELLY

Revisiting *Coming Home*

I AM GRATEFUL FOR THIS OPPORTUNITY to reflect on the central argument and related claims I put forward in *Coming Home: The Birth and Transformation of the Planetary Era* (2010). Now well into the second half of life, I am familiar with the experience of weeks, months, and years passing ever more quickly. Still, I believe it is no projection on my part to note that the general pace of change across the planet as a whole, whose acceleration I highlighted in 2010, has only continued to mount. The sense that the Earth community is rushing toward catastrophe or to some inscrutable denouement is now widespread, despite the hollow rhetoric of the proponents of business as usual.

The main task I set myself in *Coming Home* was to present, in broad outline, a speculative philosophy of history or narrative of the evolution of consciousness, with a focus on the West and its role in the birth and ongoing transformation of the Planetary Era. Beginning with the first circumnavigation of the globe some five hundred years ago, followed shortly after by the rise of modern science, of the modern nation states and their quest for global domination, then the industrial revolution, the world wars, and economic globalization, this era has been marked by the amplification and mutation of the human presence on the planet to the point where it has become a geological force in its own right. This mutation therefore includes not only the human, but in some sense the planet as a whole, which of course is what has driven much of the discourse surrounding the idea of the Anthropocene.

I included the word *home* in the title for the various layers that inform its multivalent meaning. At its base is the idea of the place where one lives or dwells. It carries the sense of where we come from, where our roots lie, but also where we feel most truly ourselves, and thus also where we most belong. In this sense home is also symbolic of the set of values to which we attach our ultimate concern. From a metaphysical perspective, home is a symbol of both the ground and lure, the origins and destiny of consciousness. In Jungian terms, it suggests the true Self. It evokes Jean Gebser's "ever-present Origin" (*Ursprung*), Hegel's Absolute Spirit, the true Buddha nature and the Atman-Brahman of the Vedic tradition, the classical Chinese *Tao*, the ancient Greek *Logos*, the Biblical Eden and the New Jerusalem. More concretely, and most consequentially, however, it points to Gaia, our *Oikos* (from the Greek for "house" or "household," and present in the words *eco*logy and *eco*nomy), this living planet in and through whom we have our being.

If Gaia is our home, clearly in one sense we have never left it, the remarkable achievements of the space program notwithstanding. We have, however, broken with the ways of Gaia in how we live our lives, in how we organize and sustain our societies, and in the set of dominant symbols and values by which our planetary civilization has been guided. While some might want to push this break all the way back to the invention of agriculture or even further to the domestication of fire, we can at least grant that, with the advent of the Great Acceleration after the second World War, the human species—or more precisely, the so-called developed world, dragging the rest behind it—set itself on a straight track to ecological overshoot and civilizational collapse. Not long after, and in response to growing awareness of the track taken, we see the birth of the environmental movement and the first Earth Day (1970) which formalize and expand the earlier and more localized efforts on behalf of mere conservation.

The environmental movement of the late 60's and early 70's can be seen as an expression of the wider protest of the 60's Counterculture, which, broadly defined, also included the rise of feminism, the push for sexual liberation, consciousness exploration, and the Civil Rights and anti-war movements. As I argued in *Coming Home*, the deeper spirit of the 60's Counterculture was continuous with the earlier protest movement of Romanticism and philosophical Idealism (c. 1780–1830), which for their part had taken up core elements from Renaissance esotericism and medieval and ancient mystical theologies. Summarizing my main argument in the Introduction, I wrote that

we can see the relation of the dominant to this countercultural stream of the Western worldview as an expression of a deep, dialectical/dialogical and evolutionary pattern. This pattern can be described as a spiral embedded in an arc, or more precisely, a series of ever smaller arcs. The spiral reproduces the triphasic pulse of the arc (beginning, zenith, end), with each iteration happening in a shorter time span: a tightening spiral. The largest arc corresponds to the movement from the Alpha of human origins to an Omega that promises the possible stabilization of a truly planetary culture. The next shorter arc shares the same end but begins with the historical period. The third arc, always with the same end, begins with the Axial Period. First proposed by the philosopher Karl Jaspers, the Axial Period, in its principal phase, ranges from 800 to 200 BCE. In a manner resonant with the mysterious origin itself, this period saw the roughly simultaneous emergence of almost all of the world's great traditions of deep and abiding wisdom, including the first Greek philosophers (from Thales and Pythagoras to Plato and Aristotle), the Buddha, Mahavira, the writing of the Bhagavad-Gita, Zoroaster, Confucius and Lao Tsu, and the great Jewish prophets (from Isaiah to Ezekiel)....

Both the diminishing span of the arcs and the tightening spiral point to the acceleration of the time sense that is so familiar and often disquieting to us as we age. This sense of acceleration, however, has become epidemic in Western, and increasingly global, culture at large. Does this mean that the culture is growing old and nearing its end? Many believe so, and even wish it to be so, given how unsustainable it has become. There are compelling reasons to accept that we are indeed already upon the threshold that marks the end of the overlapping but increasingly shorter trajectories leading to our present moment: the historical period as a whole (5000 years),[1] the period coinciding with the rise of the West (1000 years), modernity (500 years), the age of unchecked industrial growth (200 years).

II

II

II

I   I   I   III

ORIGIN   Historical   Axial   Modernity/Planetary Era   GOAL
           Period   Period

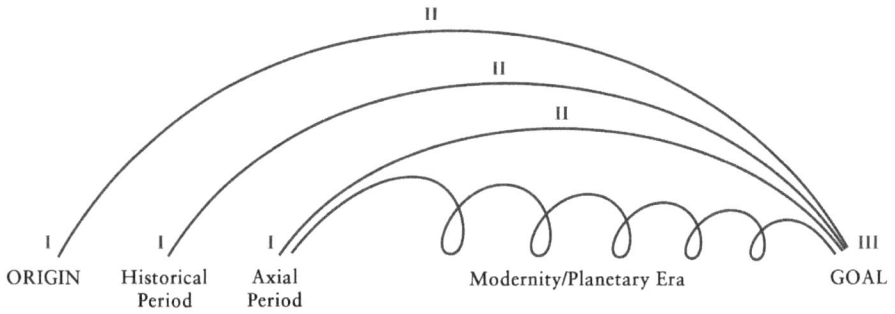

I turn now to a consideration of the Epilogue of *Coming Home* in light of the intervening years. I have inserted a few explanatory passages adapted from the body of the book, along with commentary from the perspective of 2024. The latter will appear indented and between solid lines.

Epilogue

What would it mean for us truly to come home? How would we know we had arrived? For the indigenous mind, home was a definite place (often as small as a village, sometimes as large as a bioregion), the place of one's ancestors, the stories of whose founding actions served as guidelines and regulators for sustainable living, as stores of practical knowledge and wisdom for both individuals and the community. This place was imagined as the center of the world, just as one's clan or tribe provided the type for what it meant to be human. Despite the archetypal themes underlying them, these myths—and thus also the typical human which they defined—were as numerous as the groups within which they originated. Still, "home"—or rather, the many homes—were rooted in the life of the Earth, in the cycles of the seasons and the constant rhythm of the passing generations.

With the birth of the historical period, and especially following the first Axial Period, one sees the emergence of new, more universalizing myths and cosmologies. A new tension is also introduced: on the one hand, a complexification of the older, earth-based orientation, now harmonized within the life-cycles of cultivated plants; on the other hand, a preoccupation with notions of the afterlife, with a transcendent beyond most commonly associated with the heavens—whether with the sun or the stars, in either case suggesting a realm of eternity or permanence in contrast to the changeable and death-ridden human condition and of all of life below the sphere of the moon.

Among the many mytho-cosmological visions that arose on the planet following the first Axial Period, it was the Biblical mythos which happened to serve as the Great Code [in the words of William Blake] for the eventual birth of the Planetary Era. For a thousand years prior to this birth, the West envisioned its true home along the lines of the New Jerusalem of *Revelation* or the beatific vision of Dante's *Paradiso*. By the sixteenth century, however, Renaissance humanism, the Copernican revolution, the Protestant Reformation, and the "discovery" of the New World all point to that epochal shift in axes from the vertical to the horizontal, from Heaven to Earth, which characterizes the transition to the Planetary Era.[2] Idealized in visionary utopias—Bacon's *New Atlantis*, Andrae's *Christianapolis*, Campanella's *City of the Sun*, More's *Utopia*—the New Jerusalem is now to be sought this side of the Millennium, and notably on the other side of the Atlantic.

This impetus culminates in the three great early revolutions (British, American, and French) that lead to the first modern democratic republics, two of which having their own versions of a sacred-secular trinity (life, liberty, and happiness for the Americans; liberty, equality, and fraternity for the French). In little more than a century, however, these and other fledgling states are swept up in the planetary paroxysms of two world wars, the second of which, with the onset of the nuclear age, unites the planet beneath the specter of human-generated apocalypse. A mere quarter of a century later, the world awakens to the growing ecological crisis, which, in the first decades of this new millennium, holds the real possibility of a mass extinction of species and generalized ecological and civilizational collapse.

In this critical phase of the Planetary Era, we are faced with the most extreme and fateful of contradictions: alongside the threat to the biosphere, and stimulated by this threat, and again both despite and in compensation for the newly aggravated danger of nuclear war and deepening ideological and socio-economic divisions, there are such manifestations of a truly planetary, because potentially sustainable, Earth Community as the Earth Charter, increasing international cooperation (however hobbled), and the growing populist and progressive influence of internet-facilitated democracy.

~

Some few months following the publication of Coming Home, and catalyzed by the Great Recession which began a couple of years prior, a wave of anti-austerity protests swept across the globe, culminating first in the massive mobilizations of the Arab Spring, then in the wider and more enduring Occupy movement. These protests and the movements that arose out of them, of course, were successfully repressed, co-opted, or otherwise neutralized. It is worth noting that, with respect to the Arab Spring, several of the countries where they flourished have since been devastated by US-led or assisted military interventions (Lybia, Syria, Yemen).

~

There are also the hundreds of thousands of (as yet non- or barely associated) progressive organizations around the planet which Paul Hawken has identified as the largest social movement in history, and which I call the movement for Global Solidarity. When the New Paradigm and New Age (broadly defined) groups that focus more on the psycho-spiritual dimensions of individual and global transformation are added into the equation—some notable examples include the *Institute of Noetic Sciences* (IONS), the *International Transpersonal Association*, the *Scientific and Medical Network*—the movement, already the largest ever, suddenly doubles in size.

As is the case with the swelling number of groups identified by Hawken, there is as yet no widely used name for this largest ever social movement.[3] For our purposes, we can identify it as the movement toward a *planetary wisdom culture*.

~

In the final chapter of Coming Home, I proposed four planetary ideals (cosmic solidarity, human unity, radical interdependence, and spiritual liberation) which might guide such a planetary wisdom culture. These ideals are all expressions of a deeper intuition of wholeness, which, to rise to the level of wisdom, I proposed must be coupled with the idea of complexity. My understanding of the latter drew from complexity thinker, Edgar Morin. I had first articulated the principle of *complex holism* in connection with the dialogical encounter between Hegel and Jung which I undertook in my first book, *Individuation and the Absolute*. Despite significant differences in their methods and fundamental presuppositions, Hegel and Jung both invoke the same sense of wholeness as a kind of highest value. This wholeness, however, is no mere featureless, non-dual totality. It is complex, which is to say that it includes difference and the tension of opposites. In Morin's terms, it is dialogical (nourished by the tension of opposites), recursive (recognizes feedback loops or circular causality), holographic (where parts and whole are mutually constitutive), and uncertain. It is the kind of wholeness that we see at work in all living or self-organizing systems, in everything from cells to suns, from the individual psyche to Gaia. If the many seeds of a planetary wisdom culture are to continue to bear fruit, much will depend upon the degree to which the programs, platforms, and strategies embraced by the various communities which nurture these seeds are in alignment not only with the above-mentioned planetary ideals (or their analogues) but with the more fundamental principle of complex holism, especially as the latter is embodied in the self-organizing character of the living body of Gaia.

~

This is not to say that all or even most of these groups would embrace or enact the principle of complex holism articulated in the last chapter [of *Coming Home*]. The majority of them would, however, affirm some version of the four planetary ideals of cosmic solidarity, human unity, radical interdependence, and spiritual liberation with which I illustrated the nature and virtue of this principle. This emergent planetary wisdom culture is the latest flowering—and really the first to surface on a planetary scale—of the periodic countercultural impulse which has played such a key role in the birth and transformation of the Planetary Era. Hawken invokes Gary Snyder's image of the "great underground" to characterize this impulse. Its lineage "can be traced back to healers, priestesses, philosophers, monks, rabbis, poets, and artists 'who speak for the planet, for other species, for interdependence, a life that courses under and through and around empires.'"[4] This time, however, the movement cannot go under—unless, that is, we are prepared to see civilization itself and the biosphere as it has existed for many thousands, if not millions of years, go under along with it.

If a truly planetary wisdom culture does succeed in fully emerging and stabilizing itself, there will be much that *must* go under: business as usual, industrial growth society, unchecked corporate rule, unsustainable modes of production and consumption, the roguery of nations, to name the most obvious. We could also say that what must go under is *Empire*—a term, following David Korten's usage, that refers to "the hierarchical ordering of human relationships based on the principle of domination." More particularly, the spirit of Empire "embraces material excess for the ruling classes, honors the dominator power of death and violence, denies the feminine principle, and suppresses the realization of the potentials of human maturity."[5] The antidote to Empire, according to Korten (who adopts the phrase from Brian Swimme and Thomas Berry), is *Earth Community*, which stands for "the egalitarian democratic ordering of relationships based on the principle of partnership." The spirit of Earth Community "embraces material sufficiency for everyone, honors the generative power of life and love, seeks a balance of feminine and masculine principles, and nurtures a realization of the mature potential of our human nature."[6]

To describe the shift towards Earth Community, Korten follows Joanna Macy's evocation of "The Great Turning," an image that harmonizes with the spiraling character of the fundamental pattern over the last two thousand years, as well as with the promise of a Second Axial Period.

~

In Macy's understanding, there are three dimensions to the Great Turning, all of which are forms of engagement, and therefore of activism, though the first dimension—Holding Actions in defense of the greater Earth Community—is what most people associate with the notion of activism. Such actions aim to hold back and slow down the damage being caused by the political economy of Business as Usual and can take political, legislative and legal form, as well as direct actions. The second dimension—Life-Sustaining Systems and Practices—has two complementary sides, a critical and a constructive. The critical side takes the form of "analysis of the structural causes" of our planetary predicament, and an uncovering of the dynamics of Industrial Growth Society and its plagues: ecospheric devastation, social injustice, psychosocial and spiritual malaise. The constructive side involves the "creation of alternatives" to current social, economic, political, legal, and educational arrangements—including renewable energy, regenerative design, permaculture, Earth law, local currencies, coops, and too many more to list here.

The third dimension—Shift in Consciousness—is generally implicit in the first two dimensions, but must be made explicit for them to be fully coherent and sustainable. This shift involves uncovering and cultivating our deeper identities as actors in the grand evolutionary adventure of ongoing cosmogenesis and as vehicles for the emergent self-consciousness of Gaia. It means embracing multiple ways of knowing—holistic, systemic, and complex; imaginal and poetic; emotional and embodied. It means waking up to, and celebrating, our radical inter-being, our inseverable participation in the sacred web of life, affirming and enacting our solidarity with all members of the Earth community, knowing that "everything that lives is holy" (Blake).

The teaching and practice of the Great Turning is a powerful embodiment of a planetary wisdom culture. It is also a leading expression of the second Axial Age unfolding in our time. While the first Axial Age was universal in aspiration, its exponents were still caught in forms of ethno-linguistic exclusivism. The various articulations of the universal also tended to emphasize the vertical axis of transcendence (redemption from the "vale of tears", liberation from samsara, access to the realm of eternal forms, etc.). Expressions of the second Axial Age, for their part, are explicitly inter- and multi-cultural and often multi- and even meta-perspectival. In contrast to the predominantly abstract universality of the first Axial age, the second is concretely universal, honoring and grounding itself in this living planet as our true and only home. One can point to the emerging field of religion and ecology (and the greening of the world religions), to the revival and increasing cross-pollination among the world's indigenous traditions, and to the pronounced ecological dimension of the current psychedelic revival as signal expressions of the second Axial age.

~

If we succeed in making this Great (that is, planetary) Turning, the "great underground" will no longer need, or be forced, to go under. In this sense, the countercultural impulse—or the core values it has embodied—will cease being countercultural, since they will no longer be defined in opposition to the dominant culture. The Great Turning thus coincides with the final turn of the spiral, at once the *kairos* or unique and opportune moment, and the *eschaton* or terminus of the multiple converging arcs leading to and through the Planetary Era. We can expect the presence of this extended moment to be intensifying over the next decade or so.

~

As indeed it has. On the one hand, there has been an intensification of the reality and awareness of planetary interdependence. Admittedly, this intensification has been carried mostly by awareness of accelerating threats, primarily global warming (through extreme weather or climate chaos, climate refugees, the melting Artic, unprecedented wildfires, disruptions in food production), but also financial instability, renewed threat of nuclear war and nuclear contamination (Fukushima), and the accelerating mass extinction (death of the coral reefs, ocean acidification, insect apocalypse, etc.). The sudden rise of the COVID-19 global pandemic has revealed in its own way just how vulnerable industrial civilization is to collapse. Though highlighting the reality of planetary interdependence, these developments have yet to constellate a coherent or robust amplification of a planetary wisdom culture, though we can take the various proposals for some kind of "Green New Deal" as indications of movement in this direction. Coming from the grassroots level, perhaps the most notable contemporary manifestations of resistance to Business as Usual are the Extinction Rebellion (XR) and Youth Climate Movements. What is most striking about these movements is, first, their planetary scope, and second, the fact that they explicitly acknowledge the imminent existential threat that confronts the entire Earth community.

~

Some futurists point to the imminence of a technological Singularity—Ray Kurzweil, most famously, has fixed its arrival to around 2035—which promises sweeping revolutions not only in communications, computation, energy use, bio-engineering, and applied consciousness research, but in the ability to manage more effectively the physical complexities and challenges of the Planetary Era (ecosystem and resource management).[7] The Singularity theorists, however, generally neglect to factor in the economic and political realities, let alone the deeper paradigmatic assumptions of Empire that drive these realities. In any case, we may not have until 2035. At least with respect to global climate change and the current mass extinction, we would seem to have about a five-year window (from the time of writing), centering therefore around the widely charged 2012 (the eschaton of the Mayan calendar's "Great Count" of roughly five thousand years), before the tipping points are irrevocably passed.

~

As with the widespread anticipation of Y2K at the turn of the millennium, the end of the Mayan Great Count has come and gone without the planetary apocalypse that many had anticipated. In 2018, however, the United Nations and the IPCC warned that we had only *twelve years* left to do what is necessary to avoid irreversible climate catastrophe. Others were less optimistic (if I can even use that word in this context), warning that we only have [now "had"] until 2020 to implement the needed changes.[8]

~

There is neither stopping nor turning back. Though it is impossible to say with certainty how those on the other side of the Great Turning—the sustainers of a planetary wisdom culture—will name or come to define themselves, we can expect their founders and the transformative communities they inspire to share certain essential elements or qualities with all preceding countercultural turns of the tightening spiral: something resonant with the charismatic communalism of the early Christian community, with the liberatory aspirations of the Joachimites and spiritual Franciscans, the theo-cosmic vision of the Renaissance magi and utopians, the organicist and re-enchanted worldview of the Romantics and Idealists (and the esoteric streams from which they drew), and the countercultural breakthroughs of the last century, especially those associated with the sixties Counterculture and the New Paradigm movement that followed. There will also, no doubt, be novel manifestations of the emergent planetary spirit which, though they can be imagined and even cultivated, will only be definitively recognized after the fact.

~

Alongside the XR and Youth Climate movements, which in terms of Macy's model of the Great Turning fall mostly into the category of Holding Actions (even if their adherents are also strong advocates for the adoption of alternative, Life-Sustaining Structures), there are indications as well of an intensified Shift in Consciousness in many domains, many of which represent a rekindling of movements which surfaced with great intensity during the 60s. I have already mentioned the psychedelic renaissance. No one could have imagined ten years ago that, within the decade, cannabis would be legalized and that the federal government would allow the resumption of research into the therapeutic value Schedule One substances (MDMA, psilocybin). Moving from the psychospiritual realm to that of social justice, two major waves of activism have emerged over the last decade which also link back to the 60s:

#Black Lives Matter, which revitalized the African American roots of the Civil Rights movement, and more the more generalized anti-racism movement; and the #Me Too movement, which can be seen as a new wave of the Women's Liberation Movement (itself catalyzed by the Civil Rights movement).

~

"Beneath the crust of visible reality," writes Morin, "there is a subterranean and occult reality that will emerge later but that remains completely invisible to the realist."[9]

Still, from the simultaneously open and bounded perspective of that learned ignorance[10] by which the new spirit must be guided, we must face the possibility that the Planetary Era "may ... come to naught before it has even begun to bloom. Perhaps humankind's struggles may lead only to death and ruin." "However," Morin adds, "the worst is not yet certain, and the game is not yet over. In the absence of any certainty or even probability, there is the possibility of a better world."[11]

~

In all honesty, the past few years have eroded the sense I had of what was still possible (if unlikely) in 2010. I still believe in the possibility of avoiding the worst, and given the inescapable uncertainty that attaches to all complex systems, I happily leave room for the unexpected. At the same time, I have come to accept that, in all likelihood, we will not be able to halt the Great Unraveling (that is, the mass extinction of species underway; though we may still be able to limit its extent). I have also come to accept the inevitability of civilizational collapse, which should not be surprising if one realizes that civilizations depend upon a complex and resilient enough biotic environment for their material needs, their so-called ecosystem services. We cannot know when or how soon collapse will happen—where it has not already happened, or is not already happening, that is—just as we cannot know how many species of complex life might survive, and for how long, if we do manage to avoid the worst. What we do know is that, for now at least, there are still species that *might* be saved. There are habitats that *might* be preserved. And for now, at least, there is still much that can be done not only to protect, but to regenerate habitats. There is still much that can be done, and doubtless will need to be done, to alleviate the suffering of our own species, too many of whom are caught in lives of relentless suffering.

Much like Pascal's wager, when he imagined being faced with only a vanishingly small chance (or even *apparently* none at all) of eternal salvation, the stakes are now so high that everything must be done "as if" there were a chance, if not to achieve previously cherished utopian visions, then at least to avoid the worst. And we always have the chance to avoid the worst, since the worst is perhaps nothing other than the refusal to see that the life and truth and justice for which we fight are absolutes in their own right, are the ends which ground and must determine the most skillful of means. Salvation, in this context, is not some promised eternal life in an otherworldly Heaven. People are still free, of course, to believe in such a Heaven. For my part, in the place of such belief, and even instead of a much reduced hope in the successful transition to some kind of planetary "ecological civilization," I have chosen to cultivate a different kind of *faith*: not a faith in otherworldly salvation or in the modern dream of endless progress, but faith in what the heart-mind can, even now, affirm as the highest good.[12] Morin captures the spirit of this good with the maxim: "*aimez pour vivre, vivez pour aimer!*"—which might be translated as: *love for the sake of life, live for the sake of love!* As for love, Morin notes that it concentrates in itself the power of "communion, enchantment, fervor, ecstasy; it lets us live the life of non-separation in separation, the life of the sacred, the adoration of a mortal, evanescent, and fragile being." He adds: "Love the fragile and perishable, for the best and most precious of things—including consciousness, beauty, and the soul—are fragile and perishable."[13] Our planet-home is perishable, as is the great Sun which it circles. To know this, and yet still to choose life and justice and love is to know at last, and against all odds, that we have truly come home.

Notes

1   By the end of the historical period, I am obviously not claiming that time is coming to an end, or that significant events will cease to transpire, or that histories will no longer be written. Neither am I necessarily invoking the Hegelian (or Kojèvian) notion of the end of history (see Kelly, 1993, especially pp.170f.), and certainly not Fukuyama's neo-liberal flattening of this notion. Rather, I am simply pointing to the fact that what has constituted the main driving force and central theme of the historical process from its inception to the present—namely, the quest for autonomy and dominance on the part of individual nations—must now give way to a growing recognition of the fact of pervasive interdependence on a planetary scale.

2   While the Copernican revolution displaced the earth in favor of the sun as the center of the observable cosmos, this displacement was the first and necessary step toward the articulation (realized by Newton) of a universal physics (unifying heaven and earth and allowing for an unprecedented manipulation of the material world). The pre-Copernican earth, though spatially central, stood at the lowest level of the ancient and medieval vertical hierarchy. In the post-Copernican cosmos, this hierarchy is leveled and all matter, celestial and terrestrial, now lies on the same (ontologically) horizontal plane.

3   Paul Ray and Sherry Anderson have suggested the term "cultural creatives" to describe this portion of the population (see Anderson and Ray, *The Cultural Creatives: How 50 Million People Are Changing the World* (Three Rivers, 2001).

4   Paul Hawken, *Blessed Unrest: How the Largest Movement in the World Came Into Being and Why No One Saw It Coming* (Viking, 2008), 5.

5   David Korten, *The Great Turning: From Empire to Earth Community* (Kumarion Press, 2006) 20.

6   *Ibid.*

7   See J. Martin, *The Meaning of the 21st Century: A Vital Blueprint for Ensuring Our Future.* New York: Riverhead Books, 2006.

8   "'The climate math is brutally clear: While the world can't be healed within the next few years, it may be fatally wounded by negligence until 2020,' said Hans Joachim Schellnhuber, founder and now director emeritus of the Potsdam Climate Institute. The sense that the end of next year is the last chance saloon for climate change is becoming clearer all the time. 'I am firmly of the view that the next 18 months will decide our ability to keep climate change to survivable levels and to

restore nature to the equilibrium we need for our survival,' said Prince Charles, speaking at a reception for Commonwealth foreign ministers recently." https://www.bbc.com/news/science-environment-48964736

9   Edgar Morin, with A.B. Kern, *Homeland Earth: A Manifesto for the New Millennium* (Kreskill, NJ: 1999), 100.

10 I am drawing here from the ideal of wisdom articulated by Nicolas of Cusa in his text, *On Learned Ignorance*, in which he explores the intuition of God or the Absolute as *complexio oppositorum*. Jung adopted the same formula for his definition of the Self as the paradoxical unity of consciousness and the (collective) unconscious.

11 *Ibid.*, 149.

12 See my the chapter "Living In End Times: Beyond Hope and Despair," in *Becoming Gaia: On the Threshold of Planetary Initiation.* (Revelore Press, 2021)

13 Edgar Morin, *La Méthode 6: Éthique* (Éditions du Seuil, 2004). pp. 157 and 232, respectively (my translation).

MUTATIONS

. . . is a metamorphic zone for cultural transformation, spiritual practice, and transdisciplinary experimentation. It is inspired by Jean Gebser's concept of worldview transformation, "mutation," Gloria Anzaldúa's Nahuatl concept of "Nepantla" (in-between') and what Gilles Deleuze has called 'the middle.'

It is only by staying in the middle of things—staying in radical relation—that our species can hope to enact habitable and planetary futures.

In the spirit of what William Irwin Thompson called *wissenkunst* ('knowledge-art'), Mutations seeks to bridge disciplines and find connections between art and science, myth and history. It is a place for creative seekers and misfits who dare to imagine alternative futures to explore how they can embody such futures in our vertiginous present.

It is a call back to soul; an intensification of creativity and consciousness at the craggy shoreline of one worldview and the quiet, but assured presence of another already beneath our feet.

This 'new' worldview is, as Donna Haraway suggests, 'tentacular,' arrayed with more than human kin and relations, and distributed diachronically across time and space.

This ground which rises to meet us is already present.

Join the Mutations community, a vibrant online community of seekers, learners, and way finders. We host annual courses, workshops, and starting in 2025, in-person events and retreats between New England and the West coast USA.

www.mutations.blog

Milton Keynes UK
Ingram Content Group UK Ltd.
UKHW050853221124
451587UK00016B/164

9 781947 544291